THE AMERICANNESS OF WALT WHITMAN

Problems in American Civilization

UNDER THE EDITORIAL DIRECTION OF *George Rogers Taylor*

THE AMERICANNESS OF
WALT WHITMAN

EDITED WITH AN INTRODUCTION BY

Leo Marx

Problems in American Civilization

D. C. HEATH AND COMPANY: Boston

ENGLEWOOD · INDIANAPOLIS · DALLAS · SAN FRANCISCO · ATLANTA

INTRODUCTION

BY now the Americanness of Walt Whitman's poetry is one of the postulates of literary discourse. It is an idea almost as axiomatic as the greatness of Shakespeare. People of every nationality, temper, and belief seem to find in Whitman the essence of the American way. Europeans are particularly fond of the idea — perhaps they are more fond of it than Americans are, but of course no one can have liked it better than Walt Whitman. (In the present collection, only George Santayana would deny the representative quality of the poetry.) When readers of Whitman get around to *naming* the American essence in the poetry, however, the agreement ends — just as it does when they try to locate Shakespeare's greatness. The native bias in Whitman has been identified with egalitarianism (both noble and vicious), democracy, expansiveness, egotism, a visionary bent, a taste for experiment, lack of refinement, hostility to traditional forms, a symbol-making imagination, mindlessness — one could go on. Today some of our critics are fascinated by affinities between Whitman's work and the mode of native humor. At any rate, whether we have a specific notion in mind or not, we can hardly avoid thinking of *Leaves of Grass* as if it bore the subtitle: "Poems — Uniquely American."

These readings have been selected to assist students in forming a more precise idea of the relation between Whitman's poetry, especially "Song of Myself," and American experience. Again, there is widespread agreement about the importance and typicality of "Song of Myself." Few critics, to be sure, would say that it is Whitman's best poem. Certainly it is not his most finished or coherent piece of work. According to current literary standards, "Song of Myself" is less successful than, say, either of the great elegies, "Out of the Cradle Endlessly Rocking" or "When Lilacs Last in the Dooryard Bloom'd." But "Song of Myself," partly because of its scope and, even more important, its theme, more fully reveals Whitman's special view of life. Besides, the poem exhibits the extraordinary range of his poetic voice, containing passages as delicate and moving as any he wrote, and others that are astonishingly crude. In short, "Song of Myself" is the poem to which statements about Whitman's Americanness most often refer.

The aim of this volume is to accompany and illuminate, not to supplant, a serious reading of Whitman's poetry. The first and most important fact about Walt Whitman is that he wrote, as Emerson put it, "an extraordinary piece of wit and wisdom." If we are interested in his Americanness it is because of the existence of the poetry and not the other way around. By rights this collection should be stamped with a warning in red, like some medications:

DANGER! POISON! DO NOT READ
CRITICISM BEFORE READING
WHITMAN!

Unless the student comes to these critical readings with some of the poetry in mind (at the very least, "Song of Myself") much of their value will be lost. The hope is that he will read the poem, set the criticism beside it, and so test its relevance and cogency for himself.

At bottom there are three kinds of question at issue here. The first kind is the standard question of all literary criticism: what is the intrinsic merit of the poetry as poetry? Does the poet succeed in using language to create an original organization of thought and feeling? The second kind of question relates the poem to time and place: what distinctive characteristics of American experience, if any, does Whitman's work embody? Are these the significant qualities of his verse? How important are they? The third kind of question brings us to the zone where literary criticism and history meet: in so far as the poem may be identified with American culture, what does it reveal about the strength or weakness of that culture? Can Whitman's poetic achievement be understood as in some sense an index of the quality of the American consciousness generally?

CONTENTS

88060

The Clash of Issues

Is Whitman's poetry characteristically American?

If some day a tourist notices, among the ruins of New York City, a copy of *Leaves of Grass*, and stops and picks it up and reads some lines in it, she will be able to say to herself: "How very American! If he and his country had not existed, it would have been impossible to imagine them."

— RANDALL JARRELL

He is surely not the spokesman of the tendencies of his country, although he describes some aspects of its past and present condition: nor does he appeal to those whom he describes, but rather to the *dilettanti* he despises. He is regarded as representative chiefly by foreigners, who look for some grotesque expression of the genius of so young and prodigious a people.

— GEORGE SANTAYANA

But Whitman, the greatest and the first and the only American teacher, was no Saviour. . . . The soul living her life along the incarnate mystery of the open road. . . . This is Whitman's essential message. . . . It is the inspiration of thousands of Americans today, the best souls of today, men and women. And it is a message that only in America can be fully understood, finally accepted.

— D. H. LAWRENCE

Is it great poetry?

I am not blind to the worth of the wonderful gift of *Leaves of Grass*, I find it the most extraordinary piece of wit and wisdom that America has yet contributed.

— RALPH WALDO EMERSON

Walt Whitman has given utterance to the soul of the tramp. . . . In Whitman's works the elemental parts of a man's mind and the fragments of imperfect education may be seen merging together, floating and sinking in a sea of insensate egotism and rhapsody, repellent, divine, disgusting, extraordinary.

— JOHN JAY CHAPMAN

Some one spoke of Whitman, and it was a joy to me to discover that [Henry] James thought him, as I did, the greatest of American poets. *Leaves of Grass* was put in his hands, and all that evening we sat rapt as he wandered from "The Song of Myself" to "When Lilacs Last . . ."

— EDITH WHARTON

This awful Whitman. This post mortem poet. This poet with the private soul leaking out of him all the time. All his privacy leaking out in a sort of dribble, oozing into the universe.

— D. H. LAWRENCE

Walt Whitman: SONG OF MYSELF

The first edition of Leaves of Grass *(1855) was a baffling volume. It was a thin, green quarto of ninety-five pages. Instead of the author's name on the title page there was a picture, on the opposite page, of a bearded, slouching fellow (Whitman) in his shirt sleeves. Almost half the volume was taken up by a long, untitled poem later called "Song of Myself." There were no section numbers to help the reader. But in what is now line 497 (the present text is taken from the 1891–2 edition) the writer identified himself as "Walt Whitman, an American." Few people had ever heard of him. But as soon as he read the poem, Ralph Waldo Emerson, one of the nation's leading men of letters, wrote to Whitman saying, "I greet you at the beginning of a great career. . . ."*

1

I celebrate myself, and sing myself,
And what I assume you shall assume,
For every atom belonging to me as good belongs to you.

I loafe and invite my soul,
I lean and loafe at my ease observing a spear of summer grass.

My tongue, every atom of my blood, form'd from this soil, this air,
Born here of parents born here from parents the same, and their parents the same,
I, now thirty-seven years old in perfect health begin,
Hoping to cease not till death.

Creeds and schools in abeyance,   10
Retiring back a while sufficed at what they are, but never forgotten,
I harbor for good or bad, I permit to speak at every hazard,
Nature without check with original energy.

2

Houses and rooms are full of perfumes, the shelves are crowded with perfumes,
I breathe the fragrance myself and know it and like it,
The distillation would intoxicate me also, but I shall not let it.

The atmosphere is not a perfume, it has no taste of the distillation, it is odorless,
It is for my mouth forever, I am in love with it,

I will go to the bank by the wood and become undisguised and naked,
I am mad for it to be in contact with me.   20

The smoke of my own breath,
Echoes, ripples, buzz'd whispers, love-root, silk-thread, crotch and vine,
My respiration and inspiration, the beating of my heart, the passing of blood and
    air through my lungs,
The sniff of green leaves and dry leaves, and of the shore and dark-color'd sea-
    rocks, and of hay in the barn,
The sound of the belch'd words of my voice loos'd to the eddies of the wind,
A few light kisses, a few embraces, a reaching around of arms,
The play of shine and shade on the trees as the supple boughs wag,
The delight alone or in the rush of the streets, or along the fields and hill-sides,
The feeling of health, the full-noon trill, the song of me rising from bed and
    meeting the sun.

Have you reckon'd a thousand acres much? have you reckon'd the earth much? 30
Have you practis'd so long to learn to read?
Have you felt so proud to get at the meaning of poems?

Stop this day and night with me and you shall possess the origin of all poems,
You shall possess the good of the earth and sun, (there are millions of suns left,)
You shall no longer take things at second or third hand, nor look through the eyes
    of the dead, nor feed on the spectres in books,
You shall not look through my eyes either, nor take things from me,
You shall listen to all sides and filter them from your self.

3

I have heard what the talkers were talking, the talk of the beginning and the end,
But I do not talk of the beginning or the end.

There was never any more inception than there is now,   40
Nor any more youth or age than there is now,
And will never be any more perfection than there is now,
Nor any more heaven or hell than there is now.

Urge and urge and urge,
Always the procreant urge of the world.
Out of the dimness opposite equals advance, always substance and increase,
    always sex,
Always a knit of identity, always distinction, always a breed of life.

To elaborate is no avail, learn'd and unlearn'd feel that it is so.

Sure as the most certain sure, plumb in the uprights, well entretied, braced in the
    beams,
Stout as a horse, affectionate, haughty, electrical,   50
I and this mystery here we stand.

Clear and sweet is my soul, and clear and sweet is all that is not my soul.

Lack one lacks both, and the unseen is proved by the seen,
Till that becomes unseen and receives proof in its turn.

Showing the best and dividing it from the worst age vexes age,
Knowing the perfect fitness and equanimity of things, while they discuss I am
   silent, and go bathe and admire myself.

Welcome is every organ and attribute of me, and of any man hearty and clean,
Not an inch nor a particle of an inch is vile, and none shall be less familiar than
   the rest.
I am satisfied — I see, dance, laugh, sing;
As the hugging and loving bed-fellow sleeps at my side through the night, and
   withdraws at the peep of the day with stealthy tread,   60
Leaving me baskets cover'd with white towels swelling the house with their plenty,
Shall I postpone my acceptation and realization and scream at my eyes,
That they turn from gazing after and down the road,
And forthwith cipher and show me to a cent,
Exactly the value of one and exactly the value of two, and which is ahead?

4

Trippers and askers surround me,
People I meet, the effect upon me of my early life or the ward and city I live in,
   or the nation,
The latest dates, discoveries, inventions, societies, authors old and new,
My dinner, dress, associates, looks, compliments, dues,
The real or fancied indifference of some man or woman I love,   70
The sickness of one of my folks or of myself, or ill-doing or loss or lack of money,
   or depressions or exaltations,
Battles, the horrors of fratricidal war, the fever of doubtful news, the fitful events;
These come to me days and nights and go from me again,
But they are not the Me myself.

Apart from the pulling and hauling stands what I am,
Stands amused, complacent, compassionating, idle, unitary,
Looks down, is erect, or bends an arm on an impalpable certain rest,
Looking with side-curved head curious what will come next,
Both in and out of the game and watching and wondering at it.

Backward I see in my own days where I sweated through fog with linguists and
   contenders,   80
I have no mockings or arguments, I witness and wait.

5

I believe in you my soul, the other I am must not abase itself to you,
And you must not be abased to the other.

Loafe with me on the grass, loose the stop from your throat,
Not words, not music or rhyme I want, not custom or lecture, not even the best,
Only the lull I like, the hum of your valvèd voice.

I mind how once we lay such a transparent summer morning,
How you settled your head athwart my hips and gently turn'd over upon me,
And parted the shirt from my bosom-bone, and plunged your tongue to my bare-
    stript heart,
And reach'd till you felt my beard, and reach'd till you held my feet.   90

Swiftly arose and spread around me the peace and knowledge that pass all the
    argument of the earth,
And I know that the hand of God is the promise of my own,
And I know that the spirit of God is the brother of my own,
And that all the men ever born are also my brothers, and the women my sisters
    and lovers,
And that a kelson of the creation is love,
And limitless are leaves stiff or drooping in the fields,
And brown ants in the little wells beneath them,
And mossy scabs of the worm fence, heap'd stones, elder, mullein and poke-weed.

6

A child said *What is the grass?* fetching it to me with full hands,
How could I answer the child? I do not know what it is any more than he.   100

I guess it must be the flag of my disposition, out of hopeful green stuff woven.

Or I guess it is the handkerchief of the Lord,
A scented gift and remembrancer designedly dropt,
Bearing the owner's name someway in the corners, that we may see and remark,
    and say *Whose?*

Or I guess the grass is itself a child, the produced babe of the vegetation.

Or I guess it is a uniform hieroglyphic,
And it means, Sprouting alike in broad zones and narrow zones,
Growing among black folk as among white,
Kanuck, Tuckahoe, Congressman, Cuff, I give them the same, I receive them the
    same.

And now it seems to me the beautiful uncut hair of graves.   110

Tenderly will I use you curling grass,
It may be you transpire from the breasts of young men,
It may be if I had known them I would have loved them,
It may be you are from old people, or from offspring taken soon out of their
    mothers' laps,
And here you are the mothers' laps.

This grass is very dark to be from the white heads of old mothers,
Darker than the colorless beards of old men,
Dark to come from under the faint red roofs of mouths.

O I perceive after all so many uttering tongues,
And I perceive they do not come from the roofs of mouths for nothing.   120

I wish I could translate the hints about the dead young men and women,
And the hints about old men and mothers, and the offspring taken soon out of their
    laps.

What do you think has become of the young and old men?
And what do you think has become of the women and children?

They are alive and well somewhere,
The smallest sprout shows there is really no death,
And if ever there was it led forward life, and does not wait at the end to arrest it,
And ceas'd the moment life appear'd.

All goes onward and outward, nothing collapses,
And to die is different from what any one supposed, and luckier.   130

7

Has any one supposed it lucky to be born?
I hasten to inform him or her it is just as lucky to die, and I know it.

I pass death with the dying and birth with the new-wash'd babe, and am not
    contain'd between my hat and boots,
And peruse manifold objects, no two alike and every one good,
The earth good and the stars good, and their adjuncts all good.

I am not an earth nor an adjunct of an earth,
I am the mate and companion of people, all just as immortal and fathomless as
    myself,
(They do not know how immortal, but I know.)

Every kind for itself and its own, for me mine male and female,
For me those that have been boys and that love women,   140

For me the man that is proud and feels how it stings to be slighted,
For me the sweet-heart and the old maid, for me mothers and the mothers of
    mothers,
For me lips that have smiled, eyes that have shed tears,
For me children and the begetters of children.

Undrape! you are not guilty to me, not stale nor discarded,
I see through the broadcloth and gingham whether or no,
And am around, tenacious, acquisitive, tireless, and cannot be shaken away.

8

The little one sleeps in its cradle,
I lift the gauze and look a long time, and silently brush away flies with my hand.

The youngster and the red-faced girl turn aside up the bushy hill,   150
I peeringly view them from the top.

The suicide sprawls on the bloody floor of the bedroom,
I witness the corpse with its dabbled hair, I note where the pistol has fallen.

The blab of the pave, tires of carts, sluff of boot-soles, talk of the promenaders,
The heavy omnibus, the driver with his interrogating thumb, the clank of the shod
    horses on the granite floor,
The snow-sleighs, clinking, shouted jokes, pelts of snow-balls,
The hurrahs for popular favorites, the fury of rous'd mobs,
The flap of the curtain'd litter, a sick man inside borne to the hospital,
The meeting of enemies, the sudden oath, the blows and fall,
The excited crowd, the policeman with his star quickly working his passage to the
    centre of the crowd,   160
The impassive stones that receive and return so many echoes,
What groans of over-fed or half-starv'd who fall sunstruck or in fits,
What exclamations of women taken suddenly who hurry home and give birth to
    babes,
What living and buried speech is always vibrating here, what howls restrain'd by
    decorum,
Arrests of criminals, slights, adulterous offers made, acceptances, rejections with
    convex lips,
I mind them or the show or resonance of them — I come and I depart.

9

The big doors of the country barn stand open and ready,
The dried grass of the harvest-time loads the slow-drawn wagon,
The clear light plays on the brown gray and green intertinged,
The armfuls are pack'd to the sagging mow.   170

I am there, I help, I came stretch'd atop of the load,
I felt its soft jolts, one leg reclined on the other,
I jump from the cross-beams and seize the clover and timothy,
And roll head over heels and tangle my hair full of wisps.

10

Alone far in the wilds and mountains I hunt,
Wandering amazed at my own lightness and glee,
In the later afternoon choosing a safe spot to pass the night,
Kindling a fire and broiling the fresh-kill'd game,
Falling asleep on the gather'd leaves with my dog and gun by my side.

The Yankee clipper is under her sky-sails, she cuts the sparkle and scud,   180
My eyes settle the land, I bend at her prow or shout joyously from the deck.

The boatmen and clam-diggers arose early and stopt for me,
I tuck'd my trowser-ends in my boots and went and had a good time;
You should have been with us that day round the chowder-kettle.

I saw the marriage of the trapper in the open air in the far west, the bride was a
    red girl,
Her father and his friends sat near cross-legged and dumbly smoking, they had
    moccasins to their feet and large thick blankets hanging from their shoulders,
On a bank lounged the trapper, he was drest mostly in skins, his luxuriant beard
    and curls protected his neck, he held his bride by the hand,
She had long eyelashes, her head was bare, her coarse straight locks descended
    upon her voluptuous limbs and reach'd to her feet.

The runaway slave came to my house and stopt outside,
I heard his motions crackling the twigs of the woodpile,   190
Through the swung half-door of the kitchen I saw him limpsy and weak,
And went where he sat on a log and led him in and assured him,
And brought water and fill'd a tub for his sweated body and bruis'd feet,
And gave him a room that enter'd from my own, and gave him some coarse clean
    clothes,
And remember perfectly well his revolving eyes and his awkwardness,
And remember putting plasters on the galls of his neck and ankles;
He staid with me a week before he was recuperated and pass'd north,
I had him sit next me at table, my fire-lock lean'd in the corner.

11

Twenty-eight young men bathe by the shore,
Twenty-eight young men and all so friendly;   200
Twenty-eight years of womanly life and all so lonesome.

She owns the fine house by the rise of the bank,
She hides handsome and richly drest aft the blinds of the window.

Which of the young men does she like the best?
Ah the homeliest of them is beautiful to her.

Where are you off to, lady? for I see you,
You splash in the water there, yet stay stock still in your room.

Dancing and laughing along the beach came the twenty-ninth bather,
The rest did not see her, but she saw them and loved them.

The beards of the young men glisten'd with wet, it ran from their long hair,   210
Little streams pass'd all over their bodies.

An unseen hand also pass'd over their bodies,
It descended tremblingly from their temples and ribs.

The young men float on their backs, their white bellies bulge to the sun, they do
    not ask who seizes fast to them,
They do not know who puffs and declines with pendant and bending arch,
They do not think whom they souse with spray.

12

The butcher-boy puts off his killing-clothes, or sharpens his knife at the stall in
    the market,
I loiter enjoying his repartee and his shuffle and break-down.

Blacksmiths with grimed and hairy chests environ the anvil,
Each has his main-sledge, they are all out, there is a great heat in the fire.   220

From the cinder-strew'd threshold I follow their movements,
The lithe sheer of their waists plays even with their massive arms,
Overhand the hammers swing, overhand so slow, overhand so sure,
They do not hasten, each man hits in his place.

13

The negro holds firmly the reins of his four horses, the block swags underneath
    on its tied-over chain,
The negro that drives the long dray of the stone-yard, steady and tall he stands
    pois'd on one leg on the string-piece,
His blue shirt exposes his ample neck and breast and loosens over his hip-band,
His glance is calm and commanding, he tosses the slouch of his hat away from his
    forehead,
The sun falls on his crispy hair and mustache, falls on the black of his polish'd and
    perfect limbs.

I behold the picturesque giant and love him, and I do not stop there,   230
I go with the team also.

In me the caresser of life wherever moving, backward as well as forward sluing,
To niches aside and junior bending, not a person or object missing,
Absorbing all to myself and for this song.

Oxen that rattle the yoke and chain or halt in the leafy shade, what is that you
    express in your eyes?
It seems to me more than all the print I have read in my life.

My tread scares the wood-drake and wood-duck on my distant and day-long
    ramble,
They rise together, they slowly circle around.

I believe in those wing'd purposes,
And acknowledge red, yellow, white, playing within me,   240
And consider green and violet and the tufted crown intentional,
And do not call the tortoise unworthy because she is not something else,
And the jay in the woods never studied the gamut, yet trills pretty well to me,
And the look of the bay mare shames silliness out of me.

14

The wild gander leads his flock through the cool night,
Ya-honk he says, and sounds it down to me like an invitation,
The pert may suppose it meaningless, but I listening close,
Find its purpose and place up there toward the wintry sky.

The sharp-hoof'd moose of the north, the cat on the house-sill, the chickadee, the
    prairie-dog,
The litter of the grunting sow as they tug at her teats,   250
The brood of the turkey-hen and she with her half-spread wings,
I see in them and myself the same old law.

The press of my foot to the earth springs a hundred affections,
They scorn the best I can do to relate them.

I am enamour'd of growing out-doors,
Of men that live among cattle or taste of the ocean or woods,
Of the builders and steerers of ships and the wielders of axes and mauls, and the
    drivers of horses,
I can eat and sleep with them week in and week out.

What is commonest, cheapest, nearest, easiest, is Me,
Me going in for my chances, spending for vast returns,   260

Adorning myself to bestow myself on the first that will take me,
Not asking the sky to come down to my good will,
Scattering it freely forever.

15

The pure contralto sings in the organ loft,
The carpenter dresses his plank, the tongue of his foreplane whistles its wild
    ascending lisp,
The married and unmarried children ride home to their Thanksgiving dinner,
The pilot seizes the king-pin, he heaves down with a strong arm,
The mate stands braced in the whale-boat, lance and harpoon are ready,
The duck-shooter walks by silent and cautious stretches,
The deacons are ordain'd with cross'd hands at the altar,   270
The spinning-girl retreats and advances to the hum of the big wheel,
The farmer stops by the bars as he walks on a First-day loafe and looks at the
    oats and rye,
The lunatic is carried at last to the asylum a confirm'd case,
(He will never sleep any more as he did in the cot in his mother's bed-room;)
The jour printer with gray head and gaunt jaws works at his case,
He turns his quid of tobacco while his eyes blurr with the manuscript;
The malform'd limbs are tied to the surgeon's table,
What is removed drops horribly in a pail;
The quadroon girl is sold at the auction-stand, the drunkard nods by the bar-room
    stove,
The machinist rolls up his sleeves, the policeman travels his beat, the gate-keeper
    marks who pass,   280
The young fellow drives the express-wagon, (I love him, though I do not know
    him;)
The half-breed straps on his light boots to compete in the race,
The western turkey-shooting draws old and young, some lean on their rifles, some
    sit on logs,
Out from the crowd steps the marksman, takes his position, levels his piece;
The groups of newly-come immigrants cover the wharf or levee,
As the woolly-pates hoe in the sugar-field, the overseer views them from his saddle,
The bugle calls in the ball-room, the gentlemen run for their partners, the dancers
    bow to each other,
The youth lies awake in the cedar-roof'd garret and harks to the musical rain,
The Wolverine sets traps on the creek that helps fill the Huron,
The squaw wrapt in her yellow-hemm'd cloth is offering moccasins and bead-bags
    for sale,   290
The connoisseur peers along the exhibition-gallery with half-shut eyes bent
    sideways,
As the deck-hands make fast the steamboat the plank is thrown for the shore-going
    passengers,
The young sister holds out the skein while the elder sister winds it off in a ball,
    and stops now and then for the knots,

The one-year wife is recovering and happy having a week ago borne her first child,
The clean-hair'd Yankee girl works with her sewing-machine or in the factory or mill,
The paving-man leans on his two-handed rammer, the reporter's lead flies swiftly over the note-book, the sign-painter is lettering with blue and gold,
The canal boy trots on the tow-path, the book-keeper counts at his desk, the shoe-maker waxes his thread,
The conductor beats time for the band and all the performers follow him,
The child is baptized, the convert is making his first professions,
The regatta is spread on the bay, the race is begun, (how the white sails sparkle!)   300
The drover watching his drove sings out to them that would stray,
The pedler sweats with his pack on his back, (the purchaser higgling about the odd cent;)
The bride unrumples her white dress, the minute-hand of the clock moves slowly,
The opium-eater reclines with rigid head and just-open'd lips,
The prostitute draggles her shawl, her bonnet bobs on her tipsy and pimpled neck,
The crowd laugh at her blackguard oaths, the men jeer and wink to each other,
(Miserable! I do not laugh at your oaths nor jeer you;)
The President holding a cabinet council is surrounded by the great Secretaries,
On the piazza walk three matrons stately and friendly with twined arms,
The crew of the fish-smack pack repeated layers of halibut in the hold,   310
The Missourian crosses the plains toting his wares and his cattle,
As the fare-collector goes through the train he gives notice by the jingling of loose change,
The floor-men are laying the floor, the tinners are tinning the roof, the masons are calling for mortar,
In single file each shouldering his hod pass onward the laborers;
Seasons pursuing each other the indescribable crowd is gather'd, it is the fourth of Seventh-month, (what salutes of cannon and small arms!)
Seasons pursuing each other the plougher ploughs, the mower mows, and the winter-grain falls in the ground;
Off on the lakes the pike-fisher watches and waits by the hole in the frozen surface,
The stumps stand thick round the clearing, the squatter strikes deep with his axe,
Flatboatmen make fast towards dusk near the cotton-wood or pecan-trees,
Coon-seekers go through the regions of the Red river or through those drain'd by the Tennessee, or through those of the Arkansas,   320
Torches shine in the dark that hangs on the Chattahooche or Altamahaw,
Patriarchs sit at supper with sons and grandsons and great-grandsons around them,
In walls of adobie, in canvas tents, rest hunters and trappers after their day's sport,
The city sleeps and the country sleeps,
The living sleep for their time, the dead sleep for their time,
The old husband sleeps by his wife and the young husband sleeps by his wife;
And these tend inward to me, and I tend outward to them,
And such as it is to be of these more or less I am,
And of these one and all I weave the song of myself.

16

I am of old and young, of the foolish as much as the wise,   330
Regardless of others, ever regardful of others,
Maternal as well as paternal, a child as well as a man,
Stuff'd with the stuff that is coarse and stuff'd with the stuff that is fine,
One of the Nation of many nations, the smallest the same and the largest the same,
A Southerner soon as a Northerner, a planter nonchalant and hospitable down by
    the Oconee I live,
A Yankee bound my own way ready for trade, my joints the limberest joints on
    earth and the sternest joints on earth,
A Kentuckian walking the vale of the Elkhorn in my deer-skin leggings, a Louisi-
    anian or Georgian,
A boatman over lakes or bays or along coasts, a Hoosier, Badger, Buckeye;
At home on Kanadian snow-shoes or up in the bush, or with fishermen off
    Newfoundland,
At home in the fleet of ice-boats, sailing with the rest and tacking,   340
At home on the hills of Vermont or in the woods of Maine, or the Texan ranch,
Comrade of Californians, comrade of free North-Westerners, (loving their big
    proportions,)
Comrade of raftsmen and coalmen, comrade of all who shake hands and welcome
    to drink and meat,
A learner with the simplest, a teacher of the thoughtfullest,
A novice beginning yet experient of myriads of seasons,
Of every hue and caste am I, of every rank and religion,
A farmer, mechanic, artist, gentleman, sailor, quaker,
Prisoner, fancy-man, rowdy, lawyer, physician, priest.

I resist any thing better than my own diversity,
Breathe the air but leave plenty after me,   350
And am not stuck up, and am in my place.

(The moth and the fish-eggs are in their place,
The bright suns I see and the dark suns I cannot see are in their place,
The palpable is in its place and the impalpable is in its place.)

17

These are really the thoughts of all men in all ages and lands, they are not original
    with me,
If they are not yours as much as mine they are nothing, or next to nothing,
If they are not the riddle and the untying of the riddle they are nothing,
If they are not just as close as they are distant they are nothing.

This is the grass that grows wherever the land is and the water is,
This is the common air that bathes the globe.   360

18

With music strong I come, with my cornets and my drums,
I play not marches for accepted victors only, I play marches for conquer'd and
 slain persons.

Have you heard that it was good to gain the day?
I also say it is good to fall, battles are lost in the same spirit in which they are won.

I beat and pound for the dead,
I blow through my embouchures my loudest and gayest for them.

Vivas to those who have fail'd!
And to those whose war-vessels sank in the sea!
And to those themselves who sank in the sea!
And to all generals that lost engagements, and all overcome heroes!   370
And the numberless unknown heroes equal to the greatest heroes known!

19

This is the meal equally set, this the meat for natural hunger,
It is for the wicked just the same as the righteous, I make appointments with all,
I will not have a single person slighted or left away,
The kept-woman, sponger, thief, are hereby invited,
The heavy-lipp'd slave is invited, the venerealee is invited;
There shall be no difference between them and the rest.

This is the press of a bashful hand, this the float and odor of hair,
This is the touch of my lips to yours, this the murmur of yearning,
This the far-off depth and height reflecting my own face,   380
This the thoughtful merge of myself, and the outlet again.
Do you guess I have some intricate purpose?
Well I have, for the Fourth-month showers have, and the mica on the side of a
 rock has.
Do you take it I would astonish?
Does the daylight astonish? does the early redstart twittering through the woods?
Do I astonish more than they?

This hour I tell things in confidence,
I might not tell everybody, but I will tell you.

20

Who goes there? hankering, gross, mystical, nude;
How is it I extract strength from the beef I eat?   390

What is a man anyhow? what am I? what are you?

All I mark as my own you shall offset it with your own,
Else it were time lost listening to me.

I do not snivel that snivel the world over,
That months are vacuums and the ground but wallow and filth.

Whimpering and truckling fold with powders for invalids, conformity goes to the
    fourth-remov'd,
I wear my hat as I please indoors or out.
Why should I pray? why should I venerate and be ceremonious?

Having pried through the strata, analyzed to a hair, counsel'd with doctors and
    calculated close,
I find no sweeter fat than sticks to my own bones.   400

In all people I see myself, none more and not one a barley-corn less,
And the good or bad I say of myself I say of them.

I know I am solid and sound,
To me the converging objects of the universe perpetually flow,
All are written to me, and I must get what the writing means.

I know I am deathless,
I know this orbit of mine cannot be swept by a carpenter's compass,
I know I shall not pass like a child's carlacue cut with a burnt stick at night.

I know I am august,
I do not trouble my spirit to vindicate itself or be understood,   410
I see that the elementary laws never apologize,
(I reckon I behave no prouder than the level I plant my house by, after all.)

I exist as I am, that is enough,
If no other in the world be aware I sit content,
And if each and all be aware I sit content.

One world is aware and by the far largest to me, and that is myself,
And whether I come to my own to-day or in ten thousand or ten million years,
I can cheerfully take it now, or with equal cheerfulness I can wait.

My foothold is tenon'd and mortis'd in granite,
I laugh at what you call dissolution,   420
And I know the amplitude of time.

21

I am the poet of the Body and I am the poet of the Soul,
The pleasures of heaven are with me and the pains of hell are with me,

The first I graft and increase upon myself, the latter I translate into a new tongue.
I am the poet of the woman the same as the man,
And I say it is as great to be a woman as to be a man,
And I say there is nothing greater than the mother of men.

I chant the chant of dilation or pride,
We have had ducking and deprecating about enough,
I show that size is only development.   430

Have you outstript the rest? are you the President?
It is a trifle, they will more than arrive there every one, and still pass on.

I am he that walks with the tender and growing night,
I call to the earth and sea half-held by the night.

Press close bare-bosom'd night — press close magnetic nourishing night!
Night of south winds — night of the large few stars!
Still nodding night — mad naked summer night.

Smile O voluptuous cool-breath'd earth!
Earth of the slumbering and liquid trees!
Earth of departed sunset — earth of the mountains misty-topt!   440
Earth of the vitreous pour of the full moon just tinged with blue!
Earth of shine and dark mottling the tide of the river!
Earth of the limpid gray of clouds brighter and clearer for my sake!
Far-swooping elbow'd earth — rich apple-blossom'd earth!
Smile, for your lover comes.

Prodigal, you have given me love — therefore I to you give love!
O unspeakable passionate love.

22

You sea! I resign myself to you also — I guess what you mean,
I behold from the beach your crooked inviting fingers,
I believe you refuse to go back without feeling of me,   450
We must have a turn together, I undress, hurry me out of sight of the land,
Cushion me soft, rock me in billowy drowse,
Dash me with amorous wet, I can repay you.

Sea of stretch'd ground-swells,
Sea breathing broad and convulsive breaths,
Sea of the brine of life and of unshovell'd yet always-ready graves,
Howler and scooper of storms, capricious and dainty sea,
I am integral with you, I too am of one phase and of all phases.

Partaker of influx and efflux, I, extoller of hate and conciliation,
Extoller of amies and those that sleep in each others' arms.   460

I am he attesting sympathy,
(Shall I make my list of things in the house and skip the house that supports
    them?)

I am not the poet of goodness only, I do not decline to be the poet of wickedness
    also.

What blurt is this about virtue and about vice?
Evil propels me and reform of evil propels me, I stand indifferent,
My gait is no fault-finder's or rejecter's gait,
I moisten the roots of all that has grown.

Did you fear some scrofula out of the unflagging pregnancy?
Did you guess the celestial laws are yet to be work'd over and rectified?
I find one side a balance and the antipodal side a balance,   470
Soft doctrine as steady help as stable doctrine,
Thoughts and deeds of the present our rouse and early start.

This minute that comes to me over the past decillions,
There is no better than it and now.

What behaved well in the past or behaves well to-day is not such a wonder,
The wonder is always and always how there can be a mean man or an infidel.

23

Endless unfolding of words of ages!
And mine a word of the modern, the word En-Masse.

A word of the faith that never balks,
Here or henceforward it is all the same to me, I accept Time absolutely.   480
It alone is without flaw, it alone rounds and completes all.
That mystic baffling wonder alone completes all.

I accept Reality and dare not question it,
Materialism first and last imbuing.

Hurrah for positive science! long live exact demonstration!
Fetch stonecrop mixt with cedar and branches of lilac,
This is the lexicographer, this the chemist, this made a grammar of the old
    cartouches,
These mariners put the ship through dangerous unknown seas,
This is the geologist, this works with the scalpel, and this is a mathematician.

Gentlemen, to you the first honors always!   490
Your facts are useful, and yet they are not my dwelling,
I but enter by them to an area of my dwelling.

Less the reminders of properties told my words,
And more the reminders they of life untold, and of freedom and extrication,
And make short account of neuters and geldings, and favor men and women fully
    equipt,
And beat the gong of revolt, and stop with fugitives and them that plot and
    conspire.

24

Walt Whitman, a kosmos, of Manhattan the son,
Turbulent, fleshy, sensual, eating, drinking and breeding,
No sentimentalist, no stander above men and women or apart from them,
No more modest than immodest.   500

Unscrew the locks from the doors!
Unscrew the doors themselves from their jambs!

Whoever degrades another degrades me,
And whatever is done or said returns at last to me.

Through me the afflatus surging and surging, through me the current and index.

I speak the pass-word primeval, I give the sign of democracy,
By God! I will accept nothing which all cannot have their counterpart of on the
    same terms.

Through me many long dumb voices,
Voices of the interminable generations of prisoners and slaves,
Voices of the diseas'd and despairing and of thieves and dwarfs,   510
Voices of cycles of preparation and accretion,
And of the threads that connect the stars, and of wombs and of the father-stuff,
And of the rights of them the others are down upon,
Of the deform'd, trivial, flat, foolish, despised,
Fog in the air, beetles rolling balls of dung.

Through me forbidden voices,
Voices of sexes and lusts, voices veil'd and I remove the veil,
Voices indecent by me clarified and transfigur'd.

I do not press my fingers across my mouth,
I keep as delicate around the bowels as around the head and heart,   520
Copulation is no more rank to me than death is.

I believe in the flesh and the appetites,
Seeing, hearing, feeling, are miracles, and each part and tag of me is a miracle.
Divine am I inside and out, and I make holy whatever I touch or am touch'd from,
The scent of these arm-pits aroma finer than prayer,
This head more than churches, bibles, and all the creeds.

If I worship one thing more than another it shall be the spread of my own body,
    or any part of it,
Translucent mould of me it shall be you!
Shaded ledges and rests it shall be you!
Firm masculine colter it shall be you!   530
Whatever goes to the tilth of me it shall be you!
You my rich blood! your milky stream pale strippings of my life!
Breast that presses against other breasts it shall be you!
My brain it shall be your occult convolutions!
Root of wash'd sweet-flag! timorous pond-snipe! nest of guarded duplicate eggs!
    it shall be you!
Mix'd tussled hay of head, beard, brawn, it shall be you!
Trickling sap of maple, fibre of manly wheat, it shall be you!
Sun so generous it shall be you!
Vapors lighting and shading my face it shall be you!
You sweaty brooks and dews it shall be you!   540
Winds whose soft-tickling genitals rub against me it shall be you!
Broad muscular fields, branches of live oak, loving lounger in my winding paths,
    it shall be you!
Hands I have taken, face I have kiss'd, mortal I have ever touch'd it, it shall be you.

I dote on myself, there is that lot of me and all so luscious,
Each moment and whatever happens thrills me with joy,
I cannot tell how my ankles bend, nor whence the cause of my faintest wish,
Nor the cause of the friendship I emit, nor the cause of the friendship I take again.

That I walk up my stoop, I pause to consider if it really be,
A morning-glory at my window satisfies me more than the metaphysics of books.

To behold the day-break!   550
The little light fades the immense and diaphanous shadows,
The air tastes good to my palate.

Hefts of the moving world at innocent gambols silently rising, freshly exuding,
Scooting obliquely high and low.

Something I cannot see puts upward libidinous prongs,
Seas of bright juice suffuse heaven.

The earth by the sky staid with, the daily close of their junction,
The heav'd challenge from the east that moment over my head,
The mocking taunt, See then whether you shall be master!

25

Dazzling and tremendous how quick the sun-rise would kill me,   560
If I could not now and always send sun-rise out of me.

We also ascend dazzling and tremendous as the sun,
We found our own O my soul in the calm and cool of the daybreak.

My voice goes after what my eyes cannot reach,
With the twirl of my tongue I encompass worlds and volumes of worlds.
Speech is the twin of my vision, it is unequal to measure itself,
It provokes me forever, it says sarcastically,
Walt you contain enough, why don't you let it out then?

Come now I will not be tantalized, you conceive too much of articulation,
Do you not know O speech how the buds beneath you are folded?   570
Waiting in gloom, protected by frost,
The dirt receding before my prophetical screams,
I underlying causes to balance them at last,
My knowledge my live parts, it keeping tally with the meaning of all things,
Happiness, (which whoever hears me let him or her set out in search of this day.)

My final merit I refuse you, I refuse putting from me what I really am,
Encompass worlds, but never try to encompass me,
I crowd your sleekest and best by simply looking toward you.

Writing and talk do not prove me,
I carry the plenum of proof and every thing else in my face,   580
With the hush of my lips I wholly confound the skeptic.

26

Now I will do nothing but listen,
To accrue what I hear into this song, to let sounds contribute toward it.

I hear bravuras of birds, bustle of growing wheat, gossip of flames, clack of sticks
    cooking my meals,
I hear the sound I love, the sound of the human voice,
I hear all sounds running together, combined, fused or following,
Sounds of the city and sounds out of the city, sounds of the day and night,
Talkative young ones to those that like them, the loud laugh of work-people at
    their meals,
The angry base of disjointed friendship, the faint tones of the sick,

The judge with hands tight to the desk, his pallid lips pronouncing a death-
    sentence,   590
The heave'e'yo of stevedores unlading ships by the wharves, the refrain of the
    anchor-lifters,
The ring of alarm-bells, the cry of fire, the whirr of swift-streaking engines and
    hose-carts with premonitory tinkles and color'd lights,
The steam-whistle, the solid roll of the train of approaching cars,
The slow march play'd at the head of the association marching two and two,
(They go to guard some corpse, the flag-tops are draped with black muslin.)

I hear the violoncello, ('tis the young man's heart's complaint,)
I hear the key'd cornet, it glides quickly through my ears,
It shakes mad-sweet pangs through my belly and breast.

I hear the chorus, it is a grand opera,
Ah this indeed is music — this suits me.   600

A tenor large and fresh as the creation fills me,
The orbic flex of his mouth is pouring and filling me full.

I hear the train'd soprano (what work with hers is this?)
The orchestra whirls me wider than Uranus flies,
It wrenches such ardors from me I did not know I possess'd them,
It sails me, I dab with bare feet, they are lick'd by the indolent waves,
I am cut by bitter and angry hail, I lose my breath,
Steep'd amid honey'd morphine, my windpipe throttled in fakes of death,
At length let up again to feel the puzzle of puzzles,
And that we call Being.   610

27

To be in any form, what is that?
(Round and round we go, all of us, and ever come back thither,)
If nothing lay more develop'd the quahaug in its callous shell were enough.

Mine is no callous shell,
I have instant conductors all over me whether I pass or stop,
They seize every object and lead it harmlessly through me.

I merely stir, press, feel with my fingers, and am happy,
To touch my person to some one else's is about as much as I can stand.

28

Is this then a touch? quivering me to a new identity,
Flames and ether making a rush for my veins,   620
Treacherous tip of me reaching and crowding to help them,

My flesh and blood playing out lightning to strike what is hardly different from
  myself,
On all sides prurient provokers stiffening my limbs,
Straining the udder of my heart for its withheld drip,
Behaving licentious toward me, taking no denial,
Depriving me of my best as for a purpose,
Unbuttoning my clothes, holding me by the bare waist,
Deluding my confusion with the calm of the sunlight and pasture-fields,
Immodestly sliding the fellow-senses away,
They bribed to swap off with touch and go and graze at the edges of me,   630
No consideration, no regard for my draining strength or my anger,
Fetching the rest of the herd around to enjoy them a while,
Then all uniting to stand on a headland and worry me.

The sentries desert every other part of me,
They have left me helpless to a red marauder,
They all come to the headland to witness and assist against me.

I am given up by traitors,
I talk wildly, I have lost my wits, I and nobody else am the greatest traitor,
I went myself first to the headland, my own hands carried me there.

You villain touch! what are you doing? my breath is tight in its throat,   640
Unclench your floodgates, you are too much for me.

29

Blind loving wrestling touch, sheath'd hooded sharp-tooth'd touch!
Did it make you ache so, leaving me?

Parting track'd by arriving, perpetual payment of perpetual loan,
Rich showering rain, and recompense richer afterward.
Sprouts take and accumulate, stand by the curb prolific and vital,
Landscapes projected masculine, full-sized and golden.

30

All truths wait in all things,
They neither hasten their own delivery nor resist it,
They do not need the obstetric forceps of the surgeon,   650
The insignificant is as big to me as any,
(What is less or more than a touch?)

Logic and sermons never convince,
The damp of the night drives deeper into my soul.

(Only what proves itself to every man and woman is so,
Only what nobody denies is so.)

A minute and a drop of me settle my brain,
I believe the soggy clods shall become lovers and lamps,
And a compend of compends is the meat of a man or woman,
And a summit and flower there is the feeling they have for each other,   660
And they are to branch boundlessly out of that lesson until it becomes omnific,
And until one and all shall delight us, and we them.

31

I believe a leaf of grass is no less than the journey-work of the stars,
And the pismire is equally perfect, and a grain of sand, and the egg of the wren,
And the tree-toad is a chef-d'oeuvre for the highest,
And the running blackberry would adorn the parlors of heaven,
And the narrowest hinge in my hand puts to scorn all machinery,
And the cow crunching with depress'd head surpasses any statue,
And a mouse is miracle enough to stagger sextillions of infidels.

I find I incorporate gneiss, coal, long-threaded moss, fruits, grains, esculent
    roots,   670
And am stucco'd with quadrupeds and birds all over,
And have distanced what is behind me for good reasons,
But call any thing back again when I desire it.

In vain the speeding or shyness,
In vain the plutonic rocks send their old heat against my approach,
In vain the mastodon retreats beneath its own powder'd bones,
In vain objects stand leagues off and assume manifold shapes,
In vain the ocean settling in hollows and the great monsters lying low,
In vain the buzzard houses herself with the sky,
In vain the snake slides through the creepers and logs,   680
In vain the elk takes to the inner passes of the woods,
In vain the razor-bill'd auk sails far north to Labrador,
I follow quickly, I ascend to the nest in the fissure of the cliff.

32

I think I could turn and live with animals, they're so placid and self-contain'd,
I stand and look at them long and long.

They do not sweat and whine about their condition,
They do not lie awake in the dark and weep for their sins,
They do not make me sick discussing their duty to God,
Not one is dissatisfied, not one is demented with the mania of owning things,
Not one kneels to another, nor to his kind that lived thousands of years ago,   690
Not one is respectable or unhappy over the whole earth.
So they show their relations to me and I accept them,
They bring me tokens of myself, they evince them plainly in their possession.

I wonder where they get those tokens,
Did I pass that way huge times ago and negligently drop them?

Myself moving forward then and now and forever,
Gathering and showing more always and with velocity,
Infinite and omnigenous, and the like of those among them,
Not too exclusive toward the reachers of my remembrancers,
Picking out here one that I love, and now go with him on brotherly terms.   700

A gigantic beauty of a stallion, fresh and responsive to my caresses,
Head high in the forehead, wide between the ears,
Limbs glossy and supple, tail dusting the ground,
Eyes full of sparkling wickedness, ears finely cut, flexibly moving.

His nostrils dilate as my heels embrace him,
His well-built limbs tremble with pleasure as we race around and return.
I but use you a minute, then I resign you, stallion,
Why do I need your paces when I myself out-gallop them?
Even as I stand or sit passing faster than you.

33

Space and Time! now I see it is true, what I guess'd at,   710
What I guess'd when I loaf'd on the grass,
What I guess'd while I lay alone in my bed,
And again as I walk'd the beach under the paling stars of the morning.

My ties and ballasts leave me, my elbows rest in sea-gaps,
I skirt sierras, my palms cover continents,
I am afoot with my vision.

By the city's quadrangular houses — in log huts, camping with lumbermen,
Along the ruts of the turnpike, along the dry gulch and rivulet bed,
Weeding my onion-patch or hoeing rows of carrots and parsnips, crossing
     savannas, trailing in forests,
Prospecting, gold-digging, girdling the trees of a new purchase,   720
Scorch'd ankle-deep by the hot sand, hauling my boat down the shallow river,
Where the panther walks to and fro on a limb overhead, where the buck turns
     furiously at the hunter,
Where the rattlesnake suns his flabby length on a rock, where the otter is feeding
     on fish,
Where the alligator in his tough pimples sleeps by the bayou,
Where the black bear is searching for roots or honey, where the beaver pats the
     mud with his paddle-shaped tail;
Over the growing sugar, over the yellow-flower'd cotton plant, over the rice in its
     low moist field,

Over the sharp-peak'd farm house, with its scallop'd scum and slender shoots from the gutters,

Over the western persimmon, over the long-leav'd corn, over the delicate blue-flower flax,

Over the white and brown buckwheat, a hummer and buzzer there with the rest,

Over the dusky green of the rye as it ripples and shades in the breeze;   730

Scaling mountains, pulling myself cautiously up, holding on by low scragged limbs,

Walking the path worn in the grass and beat through the leaves of the brush,

Where the quail is whistling betwixt the woods and the wheat-lot,

Where the bat flies in the Seventh-month eve, where the great gold-bug drops through the dark,

Where the brook puts out of the roots of the old tree and flows to the meadow,

Where cattle stand and shake away flies with the tremulous shuddering of their hides,

Where the cheese-cloth hangs in the kitchen, where andirons straddle the hearth-slab, where cobwebs fall in festoons from the rafters;

Where trip-hammers crash, where the press is whirling its cylinders,

Wherever the human heart beats with terrible throes under its ribs,

Where the pear-shaped balloon is floating aloft, (floating in it myself and looking composedly down,)

Where the life-car is drawn on the slip-noose, where the heat hatches pale-green eggs in the dented sand,

Where the she-whale swims with her calf and never forsakes it,   742

Where the steam-ship trails hind-ways its long pennant of smoke,

Where the fin of the shark cuts like a black chip out of the water,

Where the half-burn'd brig is riding on unknown currents,

Where shells grow to her slimy deck, where the dead are corrupting below;

Where the dense-starr'd flag is borne at the head of the regiments,

Approaching Manhattan up by the long-stretching island,

Under Niagara, the cataract falling like a veil over my countenance,

Upon a door-step, upon the horse-block of hard wood outside,   750

Upon the race-course, or enjoying picnics or jigs or a good game of base-ball,

At he-festivals, with blackguard gibes, ironical license, bull-dances, drinking, laughter,

At the cider-mill tasting the sweets of the brown mash, sucking the juice through a straw,

At apple-peelings wanting kisses for all the red fruit I find,

At musters, beach-parties, friendly bees, huskings, house-raisings;

Where the mocking-bird sounds his delicious gurgles, cackles, screams, weeps,

Where the hay-rick stands in the barn-yard, where the dry-stalks are scatter'd, where the brood-cow waits in the hovel,

Where the bull advances to do his masculine work, where the stud to the mare, where the cock is treading the hen,

Where the heifers browse, where geese nip their food with short jerks,

Where sun-down shadows lengthen over the limitless and lonesome prairie,   760

Where herds of buffalo make a crawling spread of the square miles far and near,
Where the humming-bird shimmers, where the neck of the long-lived swan is curving and winding,
Where the laughing-gull scoots by the shore, where she laughs her near-human laugh,
Where bee-hives range on a gray bench in the garden half hid by the high weeds,
Where band-neck'd partridges roost in a ring on the ground with their heads out,
Where burial coaches enter the arch'd gates of a cemetery,
Where winter wolves bark amid wastes of snow and icicled trees,
Where the yellow-crown'd heron comes to the edge of the marsh at night and feeds upon small crabs,
Where the splash of swimmers and divers cools the warm noon,
Where the katy-did works her chromatic reed on the walnut-tree over the well, 770
Through patches of citrons and cucumbers with silver-wired leaves,
Through the salt-lick or orange glade, or under conical firs,
Through the gymnasium, through the curtain'd saloon, through the office or public hall;
Pleas'd with the native and pleas'd with the foreign, pleas'd with the new and old,
Pleas'd with the homely woman as well as the handsome,
Pleas'd with the quakeress as she puts off her bonnet and talks melodiously,
Pleas'd with the tune of the choir of the whitewash'd church,
Pleas'd with the earnest words of the sweating Methodist preacher, impress'd seriously at the camp-meeting;
Looking in at the shop-windows of Broadway the whole forenoon, flatting the flesh of my nose on the thick plate glass,
Wandering the same afternoon with my face turn'd up to the clouds, or down a lane or along the beach,
My right and left arms round the sides of two friends, and I in the middle; 781
Coming home with the silent and dark-cheek'd bush-boy, (behind me he rides at the drape of the day,)
Far from the settlements studying the print of animals' feet, or the moccasin print,
By the cot in the hospital reaching lemonade to a feverish patient,
Nigh the coffin'd corpse when all is still, examining with a candle;
Voyaging to every port to dicker and adventure,
Hurrying with the modern crowd as eager and fickle as any,
Hot toward one I hate, ready in my madness to knife him,
Solitary at midnight in my back yard, my thoughts gone from me a long while,
Walking the old hills of Judea with the beautiful gentle God by my side, 790
Speeding through space, speeding through heaven and the stars,
Speeding amid the seven satellites and the broad ring, and the diameter of eighty thousand miles,
Speeding with tail'd meteors, throwing fire-balls like the rest,
Carrying the crescent child that carries its own full mother in its belly,
Storming, enjoying, planning, loving, cautioning,
Backing and filling, appearing and disappearing,
I tread day and night such roads.

I visit the orchards of spheres and look at the product,
And look at quintillions ripen'd and look at quintillions green.

I fly those flights of a fluid and swallowing soul,   800
My course runs below the soundings of plummets.

I help myself to material and immaterial,
No guard can shut me off, no law prevent me.

I anchor my ship for a little while only,
My messengers continually cruise away or bring their returns to me.

I go hunting polar furs and the seal, leaping chasms with a pike-pointed staff,
    clinging to topples of brittle and blue.

I ascend to the foretruck,
I take my place late at night in the crow's-nest,
We sail the arctic sea, it is plenty light enough,
Through the clear atmosphere I stretch around on the wonderful beauty,   810
The enormous masses of ice pass me and I pass them, the scenery is plain in all
    directions,
The white-topt mountains show in the distance, I fling out my fancies toward them,
We are approaching some great battle-field in which we are soon to be engaged,
We pass the colossal outposts of the encampment, we pass with steel feet and
    caution,
Or we are entering by the suburbs some vast and ruin'd city,
The blocks and fallen architecture more than all the living cities of the globe.

I am a free companion, I bivouac by invading watchfires,
I turn the bridegroom out of bed and stay with the bride myself,
I tighten her all night to my thighs and lips.

My voice is the wife's voice, the screech by the rail of the stairs,   820
They fetch my man's body up dripping and drown'd.

I understand the large hearts of heroes,
The courage of present times and all times,
How the skipper saw the crowded and rudderless wreck of the steam-ship, and
    Death chasing it up and down the storm,
How he knuckled tight and gave not back an inch, and was faithful of days and
    faithful of nights,
And chalk'd in large letters on a board, *Be of good cheer, we will not desert you;*
How he follow'd with them and tack'd with them three days and would not give
    it up,
How he saved the drifting company at last,

How the lank loose-gown'd women look'd when boated from the side of their
 prepared graves,
How the silent old-faced infants and the lifted sick, and the sharp-lipp'd unshaved
 men;   830
All this I swallow, it tastes good, I like it well, it becomes mine,
I am the man, I suffer'd, I was there.

The disdain and calmness of martyrs,
The mother of old, condemn'd for a witch, burnt with dry wood, her children
 gazing on,
The hounded slave that flags in the race, leans by the fence, blowing, cover'd with
 sweat.
The twinges that sting like needles his legs and neck, the murderous buckshot and
 the bullets
All these I feel or am.

I am the hounded slave, I wince at the bite of the dogs,
Hell and despair are upon me, crack and again crack the marksmen,
I clutch the rails of the fence, my gore dribs, thinn'd with the ooze of my skin, 840
I fall on the weeds and stones,
The riders spur their unwilling horses, haul close,
Taunt my dizzy ears and beat me violently over the head with whip-stocks.

Agonies are one of my changes of garments,
I do not ask the wounded person how he feels, I myself become the wounded
 person,
My hurts turn livid upon me as I lean on a cane and observe.

I am the mash'd fireman with breast-bone broken,
Tumbling walls buried me in their debris,
Heat and smoke I inspired, I heard the yelling shouts of my comrades,
I heard the distant click of their picks and shovels,   850
They have clear'd the beams away, they tenderly lift me forth.

I lie in the night air in my red shirt, the pervading hush is for my sake,
Painless after all I lie exhausted but not so unhappy,
White and beautiful are the faces around me, the heads are bared of their fire-caps,
The kneeling crowd fades with the light of the torches.

Distant and dead resuscitate,
They show as the dial or move as the hands of me, I am the clock myself.

I am an old artillerist, I tell of my fort's bombardment,
I am there again.

Again the long roll of the drummers,   860
Again the attacking cannon, mortars,
Again to my listening ears the cannon responsive.

I take part, I see and hear the whole,
The cries, curses, roar, the plaudits for well-aim'd shots,
The ambulanza slowly passing trailing its red drip,
Workmen searching after damages, making indispensable repairs,
The fall of grenades through the rent roof, the fan-shaped explosion,
The whizz of limbs, heads, stone, wood, iron, high in the air.

Again gurgles the mouth of my dying general, he furiously waves with his hand,
He gasps through the clot *Mind not me — mind — the entrenchments.*   870

34

Now I tell what I knew in Texas in my early youth,
(I tell not the fall of Alamo,
Not one escaped to tell the fall of Alamo,
The hundred and fifty are dumb yet at Alamo,)
'Tis the tale of the murder in cold blood of four hundred and twelve young men.

Retreating they had form'd in a hollow square with their baggage for breastworks,
Nine hundred lives out of the surrounding enemy's, nine times their number, was
    the price they took in advance,
Their colonel was wounded and their ammunition gone,
They treated for an honorable capitulation, receiv'd writing and seal, gave up their
    arms and march'd back prisoners of war.

They were the glory of the race of rangers,   880
Matchless with horse, rifle, song, supper, courtship,
Large, turbulent, generous, handsome, proud, and affectionate,
Bearded, sunburnt, drest in the free costume of hunters,
Not a single one over thirty years of age.

The second First-day morning they were brought out in squads and massacred, it
    was beautiful early summer,
The work commenced about five o'clock and was over by eight.

None obey'd the command to kneel,
Some made a mad and helpless rush, some stood stark and straight,
A few fell at once, shot in the temple or heart, the living and dead lay together,
The maim'd and mangled dug in the dirt, the new-comers saw them there,   890
Some half-kill'd attempted to crawl away,
These were despatch'd with bayonets or batter'd with the blunts of muskets,

A youth not seventeen years old seiz'd his assassin till two more came to release
    him,
The three were all torn and cover'd with the boy's blood.

At eleven o'clock began the burning of the bodies;
That is the tale of the murder of the four hundred and twelve young men.

35

Would you hear of an old-time sea-fight?
Would you learn who won by the light of the moon and stars?
List to the yarn, as my grandmother's father the sailor told it to me.

Our foe was no skulk in his ship I tell you, (said he,)   900
His was the surly English pluck, and there is no tougher or truer, and never was,
    and never will be,
Along the lower'd eve he came horribly raking us.

We closed with him, the yards entangled, the cannon touch'd,
My captain lash'd fast with his own hands.

We had receiv'd some eighteen pound shots under the water,
On our lower-gun-deck two large pieces had burst at the first fire, killing all around
    and blowing up overhead.

Fighting at sun-down, fighting at dark,
Ten o'clock at night, the full moon well up, our leaks on the gain, and five feet of
    water reported,
The master-at-arms loosing the prisoners confined in the after-hold to give them a
    chance for themselves.

The transit to and from the magazine is now stopt by the sentinels,   910
They see so many strange faces they do not know whom to trust.

Our frigate takes fire,
The other asks if we demand quarter?
If our colors are struck and the fighting done?

Now I laugh content, for I hear the voice of my little captain,
We have not struck, he composedly cries, *we have just begun our part of the
    fighting.*
Only three guns are in use,
One is directed by the captain himself against the enemy's main-mast,
Two well serv'd with grape and canister silence his musketry and clear his decks.

The tops alone second the fire of this little battery, especially the main-top,   920
They hold out bravely during the whole of the action.

Not a moment's cease,
The leaks gain fast on the pumps, the fire eats toward the powder-magazine.

One of the pumps has been shot away, it is generally thought we are sinking.

Serene stands the little captain,
He is not hurried, his voice is neither high nor low,
His eyes give more light to us than our battle-lanterns.

Toward twelve there in the beams of the moon they surrender to us.

36

Stretch'd and still lies the midnight,
Two great hulls motionless on the breast of the darkness,   930
Our vessel riddled and slowly sinking, preparations to pass to the one we have
  conquer'd,
The captain on the quarter-deck coldly giving his orders through a countenance
  white as a sheet,
Near by the corpse of the child that serv'd in the cabin,
The dead face of an old salt with long white hair and carefully curl'd whiskers,
The flames spite of all that can be done flickering aloft and below,
The husky voices of the two or three officers yet fit for duty,
Formless stacks of bodies and bodies by themselves, dabs of flesh upon the masts
  and spars,
Cut of cordage, dangle of rigging, slight shock of the soothe of waves,
Black and impassive guns, litter of powder-parcels, strong scent,
A few large stars overhead, silent and mournful shining,   940
Delicate sniffs of sea-breeze, smells of sedgy grass and fields by the shore, death-
  messages given in charge to survivors,
The hiss of the surgeon's knife, the gnawing teeth of his saw,
Wheeze, cluck, swash of falling blood, short wild scream, and long, dull, tapering
  groan,
These so, these irretrievable.

37

You laggards there on guard! look to your arms!
In at the conquer'd doors they crowd! I am possess'd!
Embody all presences outlaw'd or suffering,
See myself in prison shaped like another man,
And feel the dull unintermitted pain.

For me the keepers of convicts shoulder their carbines and keep watch,   950
It is I let out in the morning and barr'd at night.

Not a mutineer walks handcuff'd to jail but I am handcuff'd to him and walk by
  his side,

(I am less the jolly one there, and more the silent one with sweat on my twitching
   lips.)

Not a youngster is taken for larceny but I go up too, and am tried and sentenced.

Not a cholera patient lies at the last gasp but I also lie at the last gasp,
My face is ash-color'd, my sinews gnarl, away from me people retreat.

Askers embody themselves in me and I am embodied in them,
I project my hat, sit shame-faced, and beg.

38

Enough! enough! enough!
Somehow I have been stunn'd. Stand back!   960
Give me a little time beyond my cuff'd head, slumbers, dreams, gaping,
I discover myself on the verge of a usual mistake.

That I could forget the mockers and insults!
That I could forget the trickling tears and the blows of the bludgeons and
   hammers!
That I could look with a separate look on my own crucifixion and bloody crowning!

I remember now,
I resume the overstaid fraction,
The grave of rock multiplies what has been confided to it, or to any graves,
Corpses rise, gashes heal, fastenings roll from me.

I troop forth replenish'd with supreme power, one of an average unending
   procession,   970
Inland and sea-coast we go, and pass all boundary lines,
Our swift ordinances on their way over the whole earth,
The blossoms we wear in our hats the growth of thousands of years.

Eleves, I salute you! come forward!
Continue your annotations, continue your questionings.

39

The friendly and flowing savage, who is he?
Is he waiting for civilization, or past it and mastering it?

Is he some Southwesterner rais'd out-doors? is he Kanadian?
Is he from the Mississippi country? Iowa, Oregon, California?
The mountains? prairie-life, bush-life? or sailor from the sea?   980

Wherever he goes men and women accept and desire him,
They desire he should like them, touch them, speak to them, stay with them.

Behavior lawless as snow-flakes, words simple as grass, uncomb'd head, laughter,
  and naïveté,
Slow-stepping feet, common features, common modes and emanations,
They descend in new forms from the tips of his fingers,
They are wafted with the odor of his body or breath, they fly out of the glance
  of his eyes.

                                    40

Flaunt of the sunshine I need not your bask — lie over!
You light surfaces only, I force surfaces and depths also.

Earth! you seem to look for something at my hands,
Say, old top-knot, what do you want?   990

Man or woman, I might tell how I like you, but cannot,
And might tell what it is in me and what it is in you, but cannot,
And might tell that pining I have, that pulse of my nights and days.

Behold, I do not give lectures or a little charity,
When I give I give myself.

You there, impotent, loose in the knees,
Open your scarf'd chops till I blow grit within you,
Spread your palms and lift the flaps of your pockets,
I am not to be denied, I compel, I have stores plenty and to spare,
And any thing I have I bestow.   1000

I do not ask who you are, that is not important to me,
You can do nothing and be nothing but what I will infold you.

To cotton-field drudge or cleaner of privies I lean,

On his right cheek I put the family kiss,
And in my soul I swear I never will deny him.

On women fit for conception I start bigger and nimbler babes,
(This day I am jetting the stuff of far more arrogant republics.)

To any one dying, thither I speed and twist the knob of the door,
Turn the bed-clothes toward the foot of the bed,
Let the physician and the priest go home.   1010

I seize the descending man and raise him with resistless will,
O despairer, here is my neck,
By God, you shall not go down! hang your whole weight upon me.

I dilate you with tremendous breath, I buoy you up,
Every room of the house do I fill with an arm'd force,
Lovers of me, bafflers of graves.

Sleep — I and they keep guard all night,
Not doubt, not decease shall dare to lay finger upon you,
I have embraced you, and henceforth possess you to myself,
And when you rise in the morning you will find what I tell you is so.   1020

41

I am he bringing help for the sick as they pant on their backs,
And for strong upright men I bring yet more needed help.

I heard what was said of the universe,
Heard it and heard it of several thousand years;
It is middling well as far as it goes — but is that all?

Magnifying and applying come I,
Outbidding at the start the old cautious hucksters,
Taking myself the exact dimensions of Jehovah,
Lithographing Kronos, Zeus his son, and Hercules his grandson,
Buying drafts of Osiris, Isis, Belus, Brahma, Buddha,   1030
In my portfolio placing Manito loose, Allah on a leaf, the crucifix engraved,
With Odin and the hideous-faced Mexitli and every idol and image,
Taking them all for what they are worth and not a cent more,
Admitting they were alive and did the work of their days,
(They bore mites as for unfledg'd birds who have now to rise and fly and sing for
    themselves,)
Accepting the rough deific sketches to fill out better in myself, bestowing them
    freely on each man and woman I see,
Discovering as much or more in a framer framing a house,
Putting higher claims for him there with his roll'd-up sleeves driving the mallet
    and chisel,
Not objecting to special revelations, considering a curl of smoke or a hair on the
    back of my hand just as curious as any revelation,
Lads ahold of fire-engines and hook-and-ladder ropes no less to me than the gods
    of the antique wars,
Minding their voices peal through the crash of destruction,   1041
Their brawny limbs passing safe over charr'd laths, their white foreheads whole
    and unhurt out of the flames;
By the mechanic's wife with her babe at her nipple interceding for every person
    born,
Three scythes at harvest whizzing in a row from three lusty angels with shirts
    bagg'd out at their waists,
The snag-tooth'd hostler with red hair redeeming sins past and to come,

Selling all he possesses, travelling on foot to fee lawyers for his brother and sit by
    him while he is tried for forgery;
What was strewn in the amplest strewing the square rod about me, and not filling
    the square rod then,
The bull and the bug never worshipp'd half enough,
Dung and dirt more admirable than was dream'd,
The supernatural of no account, myself waiting my time to be one of the
    supremes,   1050
The day getting ready for me when I shall do as much good as the best, and be
    as prodigious;
By my life-lumps! becoming already a creator,
Putting myself here and now to the ambush'd womb of the shadows.

42

A call in the midst of the crowd,
My own voice, orotund sweeping and final.

Come my children,
Come my boys and girls, my women, household and intimates,
Now the performer launches his nerve, he has pass'd his prelude on the reeds
    within.

Easily written loose-finger'd chords — I feel the thrum of your climax and close.

My head slues round on my neck,   1060
Music rolls, but not from the organ,
Folks are around me, but they are no household of mine.

Ever the hard unsunk ground.
Ever the eaters and drinkers, ever the upward and downward sun, ever the air
    and the ceaseless tides,
Ever myself and my neighbors, refreshing, wicked, real.
Ever the old inexplicable query, ever that thorn'd thumb, that breath of itches and
    thirsts,
Ever the vexer's *hoot! hoot!* till we find where the sly one hides and bring him
    forth,
Ever love, ever the sobbing liquid of life,
Ever the bandage under the chin, ever the trestles of death.

Here and there with dimes on the eyes walking,   1070
To feed the greed of the belly the brains liberally spooning,
Tickets buying, taking, selling, but in to the feast never once going,
Many sweating, ploughing, thrashing, and then the chaff for payment receiving,
A few idly owning, and they the wheat continually claiming.

This is the city and I am one of the citizens,
Whatever interests the rest interests me, politics, wars, markets, newspapers,
   schools,
The mayor and councils, banks, tariffs, steamships, factories, stocks, stores, real
   estate and personal estate.

The little plentiful manikins skipping around in collars and tail'd coats,
I am aware who they are, (they are positively not worms or fleas,)
I acknowledge the duplicates of myself, the weakest and shallowest is deathless
   with me,   1080
What I do and say the same waits for them,
Every thought that flounders in me the same flounders in them.

I know perfectly well my own egotism,
Know my omnivorous lines and must not write any less,
And would fetch you whoever you are flush with myself.

Not words of routine this song of mine,
But abruptly to question, to leap beyond yet nearer bring;
This printed and bound book — but the printer and the printing-office boy?
The well-taken photographs — but your wife or friend close and solid in your arms?
The black ship mail'd with iron, her mighty guns in her turrets — but the pluck of
   the captain and engineers?   1090
In the houses the dishes and fare and furniture — but the host and hostess, and the
   look out of their eyes?
The sky up there — yet here or next door, or across the way?

The saints and sages in history — but you yourself?
Sermons, creeds, theology — but the fathomless human brain,
And what is reason? and what is love? and what is life?

43

I do not despise you priests, all time, the world over,
My faith is the greatest of faiths and the least of faiths,
Enclosing worship ancient and modern and all between ancient and modern,
Believing I shall come again upon the earth after five thousand years,
Waiting responses from oracles, honoring the gods, saluting the sun,   1100
Making a fetich of the first rock or stump, powowing with sticks in the circle of
   obis,
Helping the llama or brahmin as he trims the lamps of the idols,
Dancing yet through the streets in a phallic procession, rapt and austere in the
   woods a gymnosophist,
Drinking mead from the skull-cup, to Shastas and Vedas admirant, minding the
   Koran,
Walking the teokallis, spotted with gore from the stone and knife, beating the
   serpent-skin drum,

Accepting the Gospels, accepting him that was crucified, knowing assuredly that
  he is divine,
To the mass kneeling or the puritan's prayer rising, or sitting patiently in a pew,
Ranting and frothing in my insane crisis, or waiting dead-like till my spirit arouses
  me,
Looking forth on pavement and land, or outside of pavement and land,
Belonging to the winders of the circuit of circuits.   1110

One of that centripetal and centrifugal gang I turn and talk like a man leaving
  charges before a journey.

Down-hearted doubters dull and excluded,
Frivolous, sullen, moping, angry, affected, dishearten'd, atheistical,
I know every one of you, I know the sea of torment, doubt, despair and unbelief.

How the flukes splash!
How they contort rapid as lightning, with spasms and spouts of blood!

Be at peace bloody flukes of doubters and sullen mopers,
I take my place among you as much as among any,
The past is the push of you, me, all, precisely the same,
And what is yet untried and afterward is for you, me, all, precisely the same. 1120

I do not know what is untried and afterward,
But I know it will in its turn prove sufficient, and cannot fail.

Each who passes is consider'd, each who stops is consider'd, not a single one can
  it fail.

It cannot fail the young man who died and was buried,
Nor the young woman who died and was put by his side,
Nor the little child that peep'd in at the door, and then drew back and was never
  seen again,
Nor the old man who has lived without purpose, and feels it with bitterness worse
  than gall,
Nor him in the poor house tubercled by rum and the bad disorder,
Nor the numberless slaughter'd and wreck'd, nor the brutish koboo call'd the
  ordure of humanity,
Nor the sacs merely floating with open mouths for food to slip in,   1130
Nor any thing in the earth, or down in the oldest graves of the earth,
Nor any thing in the myriads of spheres, nor the myriads of myriads that inhabit
  them,
Nor the present, nor the least wisp that is known.

44

It is time to explain myself — let us stand up.

What is known I strip away,
I launch all men and women forward with me into the Unknown.
The clock indicates the moment — but what does eternity indicate?

We have thus far exhausted trillions of winters and summers,
There are trillions ahead, and trillions ahead of them.

Births have brought us richness and variety,   1140
And other births will bring us richness and variety.

I do not call one greater and one smaller,
That which fills its period and place is equal to any.

Were mankind murderous or jealous upon you, my brother, my sister?
I am sorry for you, they are not murderous or jealous upon me,
All has been gentle with me, I keep no account with lamentation,
(What have I to do with lamentation?)

I am an acme of things accomplish'd, and I an encloser of things to be.

My feet strike an apex of the apices of the stairs,
On every step bunches of ages, and larger bunches between the steps,   1150
All below duly travel'd, and still I mount and mount.

Rise after rise bow the phantoms behind me,
Afar down I see the huge first Nothing, I know I was even there,
I waited unseen and always, and slept through the lethargic mist,
And took my time, and took no hurt from the fetid carbon.

Long I was hugg'd close — long and long.

Immense have been the preparations for me,
Faithful and friendly the arms that have help'd me.

Cycles ferried my cradle, rowing and rowing like cheerful boatmen,

For room to me stars kept aside in their own rings,   1160
They sent influences to look after what was to hold me.

Before I was born out of my mother generations guided me,
My embryo has never been torpid, nothing could overlay it.

For it the nebula cohered to an orb,
The long slow strata piled to rest it on,
Vast vegetables gave it sustenance,
Monstrous sauroids transported it in their mouths and deposited it with care.
All forces have been steadily employ'd to complete and delight me,
Now on this spot I stand with my robust soul.

45

O span of youth! ever-push'd elasticity.   1170
O manhood, balanced, florid and full.

My lovers suffocate me,
Crowding my lips, thick in the pores of my skin.
Jostling me through streets and public halls, coming naked to me at night,
Crying by day Ahoy! from the rocks of the river, swinging and chirping over my
    head,
Calling my name from flower-beds, vines, tangled underbrush,
Lighting on every moment of my life,
Bussing my body with soft balsamic busses,
Noiselessly passing handfuls out of their hearts and giving them to be mine.

Old age superbly rising! O welcome, ineffable grace of dying days!   1180

Every condition promulges not only itself, it promulges what grows after and out
    of itself,
And the dark hush promulges as much as any.

I open my scuttle at night and see the far-sprinkled systems,
And all I see multiplied as high as I can cipher edge but the rim of the farther
    systems.

Wider and wider they spread, expanding, always expanding,
Outward and outward and forever outward.

My sun has his sun and round him obediently wheels,
He joins with his partners a group of superior circuit,
And greater sets follow, making specks of the greatest inside them.

There is no stoppage and never can be stoppage,   1190
If I, you, and the worlds, and all beneath or upon their surfaces, were this moment
    reduced back to a pallid float, it would not avail in the long run,
We should surely bring up again where we now stand,
And surely go as much farther, and then farther and farther.

A few quadrillions of eras, a few octillions of cubic leagues, do not hazard the span
   or make it impatient,
They are but parts, any thing is but a part.

See ever so far, there is limitless space outside of that,
Count ever so much, there is limitless time around that.

My rendezvous is appointed, it is certain,
The Lord will be there and wait till I come on perfect terms,
The great Camerado, the lover true for whom I pine will be there.   1200

46

I know I have the best of time and space, and was never measured and never will
   be measured.

I tramp a perpetual journey, (come listen all!)
My signs are a rain-proof coat, good shoes, and a staff cut from the woods,
No friend of mine takes his ease in my chair,
I have no chair, no church, no philosophy,
I lead no man to a dinner-table, library, exchange,
But each man and each woman of you I lead upon a knoll,
My left hand hooking you round the waist,
My right hand pointing to landscapes of continents and the public road.

Not I, not any one else can travel that road for you,   1210
You must travel it for yourself.

It is not far, it is within reach,
Perhaps you have been on it since you were born and did not know,
Perhaps it is everywhere on water and on land.

Shoulder your duds dear son, and I will mine, and let us hasten forth,
Wonderful cities and free nations we shall fetch as we go.
If you tire, give me both burdens, and rest the chuff of your hand on my hip,
And in due time you shall repay the same service to me,
For after we start we never lie by again.

This day before dawn I ascended a hill and look'd at the crowded heaven,   1220
And I said to my spirit *When we become the enfolders of those orbs, and the*
   pleasure and knowledge of every thing in them, shall we be fill'd and satisfied
   then?
And my spirit said *No, we but level that lift to pass and continue beyond.*

You are also asking me questions and I hear you,
I answer that I cannot answer, you must find out for yourself.

Sit a while dear son,
Here are biscuits to eat and here is milk to drink,
But as soon as you sleep and renew yourself in sweet clothes, I kiss you with a
    good-by kiss and open the gate for your egress hence.

Long enough have you dream'd contemptible dreams,
Now I wash the gum from your eyes,
You must habit yourself to the dazzle of the light and of every moment of your
    life.   1230

Long have you timidly waded holding a plank by the shore,
Now I will you to be a bold swimmer,
To jump off in the midst of the sea, rise again, nod to me, shout, and laughingly
    dash with your hair.

47

I am the teacher of athletes,
He that by me spreads a wider breast than my own proves the width of my own,
He most honors my style who learns under it to destroy the teacher.

The boy I love, the same becomes a man not through derived power, but in his
    own right,
Wicked rather than virtuous out of conformity or fear,
Fond of his sweetheart, relishing well his steak,
Unrequited love or a slight cutting him worse than sharp steel cuts,   1240
First-rate to ride, to fight, to hit the bull's eye, to sail a skiff, to sing a song or play
    on the banjo,
Preferring scars and the beard and faces pitted with small-pox over all latherers,
And those well-tann'd to those that keep out of the sun.

I teach straying from me, yet who can stray from me?
I follow you whoever you are from the present hour,
My words itch at your ears till you understand them.
I do not say these things for a dollar or to fill up the time while I wait for a boat,
(It is you talking just as much as myself, I act as the tongue of you,
Tied in your mouth, in mine it begins to be loosen'd.)

I swear I will never again mention love or death inside a house,   1250
And I swear I will never translate myself at all, only to him or her who privately
    stays with me in the open air.

If you would understand me go to the heights or water-shore,
The nearest gnat is an explanation, and a drop or motion of waves a key,
The maul, the oar, the hand-saw, second my words.

No shutter'd room or school can commune with me,
But roughs and little children better than they.

The young mechanic is closest to me, he knows me well,
The woodman that takes his axe and jug with him shall take me with him all day,
The farm-boy ploughing in the field feels good at the sound of my voice,
In vessels that sail my words sail, I go with fishermen and seamen and love
   them.   1260

The soldier camp'd or upon the march is mine,
On the night ere the pending battle many seek me, and I do not fail them,
On that solemn night (it may be their last) those that know me seek me.

My face rubs to the hunter's face when he lies down alone in his blanket,
The driver thinking of me does not mind the jolt of his wagon,
The young mother and old mother comprehend me,
The girl and the wife rest the needle a moment and forget where they are,
They and all would resume what I have told them.

48

I have said that the soul is not more than the body,
And I have said that the body is not more than the soul,   1270
And nothing, not God, is greater to one than one's self is,
And whoever walks a furlong without sympathy walks to his own funeral drest
   in his shroud,
And I or you pocketless of a dime may purchase the pick of the earth,
And to glance with an eye or show a bean in its pod confounds the learning of all
   times,
And there is no trade or employment but the young man following it may become
   a hero,
And there is no object so soft but it makes a hub for the wheel'd universe,
And I say to any man or woman, Let your soul stand cool and composed before a
   million universes.

And I say to mankind, Be not curious about God,
For I who am curious about each am not curious about God,
(No array of terms can say how much I am at peace about God and about
   death.)   1280

I hear and behold God in every object, yet understand God not in the least,
Nor do I understand who there can be more wonderful than myself.

Why should I wish to see God better than this day?
I see something of God each hour of the twenty-four, and each moment then,
In the faces of men and women I see God, and in my own face in the glass,

I find letters from God dropt in the street, and every one is sign'd by God's name,
And I leave them where they are, for I know that wheresoe'er I go,
Others will punctually come for ever and ever.

49

And as to you Death, and you bitter hug of mortality, it is idle to try to alarm me.

To his work without flinching the accoucheur comes,   1290
I see the elder-hand pressing receiving supporting,
I recline by the sills of the exquisite flexible doors,
And mark the outlet, and mark the relief and escape.

And as to you Corpse I think you are good manure, but that does not offend me,
I smell the white roses sweet-scented and growing,
I reach to the leafy lips, I reach to the polish'd breasts of melons.

And as to you Life I reckon you are the leavings of many deaths,
(No doubt I have died myself ten thousand times before.)
I hear you whispering there O stars of heaven,
O suns — O grass of graves —O perpetual transfers and promotions,   1300
If you do not say any thing how can I say any thing?

Of the turbid pool that lies in the autumn forest,
Of the moon that descends the steeps of the soughing twilight,
Toss, sparkles of day and dusk — toss on the black stems that decay in the muck,
Toss to the moaning gibberish of the dry limbs.

I ascend from the moon, I ascend from the night,
I perceive that the ghastly glimmer is noonday sunbeams reflected,
And debouch to the steady and central from the offspring great or small.

50

There is that in me — I do not know what it is — but I know it is in me.

Wrench'd and sweaty — calm and cool then my body becomes,   1310
I sleep — I sleep long.

I do not know it — it is without name — it is a word unsaid,
It is not in any dictionary, utterance, symbol.

Something it swings on more than the earth I swing on,
To it the creation is the friend whose embracing awakes me.

Perhaps I might tell more. Outlines! I plead for my brothers and sisters.

Do you see O my brothers and sisters?
It is not chaos or death — it is form, union, plan — it is eternal life — it is Happiness.

51

The past and present wilt — I have fill'd them, emptied them,
And proceed to fill my next fold of the future.   1320

Listener up there! what have you to confide to me?
Look in my face while I snuff the sidle of evening,
(Talk honestly, no one else hears you, and I stay only a minute longer.)

Do I contradict myself?
Very well then I contradict myself,
(I am large, I contain multitudes.)

I concentrate toward them that are nigh, I wait on the door-slab.

Who has done his day's work? who will soonest be through with his supper?
Who wishes to walk with me?

Will you speak before I am gone? will you prove already too late?   1330

52

The spotted hawk swoops by and accuses me, he complains of my gab and my
    loitering.

I too am not a bit tamed, I too am untranslatable,
I sound my barbaric yawp over the roofs of the world.

The last scud of day holds back for me,
It flings my likeness after the rest and true as any on the shadow'd wilds,
It coaxes me to the vapor and the dusk.

I depart as air, I shake my white locks at the runaway sun,
I effuse my flesh in eddies, and drift it in lacy jags.

I bequeath myself to the dirt to grow from the grass I love,
If you want me again look for me under your boot-soles.   1340

You will hardly know who I am or what I mean,
But I shall be good health to you nevertheless,
And filter and fibre your blood.
Failing to fetch me at first keep encouraged,
Missing me one place search another,
I stop somewhere waiting for you.

Alexis de Tocqueville:
POETRY IN A DEMOCRATIC SOCIETY

When the young Frenchman, Alexis de Tocqueville (1805–1859), visited America in 1831, Walt Whitman was twelve years old, the first edition of Leaves of Grass *was twenty-four years away, and no poetry like Whitman's ever had been published anywhere. Yet Tocqueville, after nine months in the United States, came close to predicting the distinctive qualities of "Song of Myself." He said that the young republic did not have any poetry worthy of the name, but he tried to imagine what it would be like when it appeared. Of course his prophecy was no miracle. In his travels he encountered many of the men and ideas that would shape Whitman's imagination. Nevertheless, it is difficult to account for Tocqueville's prescience without acknowledging a vital relation between Whitman's poetry and the conditions of life in America.*

OF SOME SOURCES OF POETRY AMONG DEMOCRATIC NATIONS

Many different significations have been given to the word *Poetry*. It would weary my readers if I were to lead them to discuss which of these definitions ought to be selected: I prefer telling them at once that which I have chosen. In my opinion, Poetry is the search after, and the delineation of, the Ideal.

The Poet is he who, by suppressing a part of what exists, by adding some imaginary touches to the picture, and by combining certain real circumstances that do not in fact happen together, completes and extends the work of nature. Thus the object of poetry is not to represent what is true, but to adorn it and to present to the mind some loftier image. Verse, regarded as the ideal beauty of language, may be eminently poetical; but verse does not of itself constitute poetry.

I now proceed to inquire whether, amongst the actions, the sentiments, and the opinions of democratic nations there are any which lead to a conception of the ideal, and which may for this reason be considered as natural sources of poetry.

It must, in the first place, be acknowledged that the taste for ideal beauty, and the pleasure derived from the expression of it, are never so intense or so diffused amongst a democratic as amongst an aristocratic people. In aristocratic nations it sometimes happens that the body acts as it were spontaneously, whilst the higher faculties are bound and burdened by repose. Amongst these nations the people will often display poetic tastes, and their fancy sometimes ranges beyond and above what surrounds them.

But in democracies the love of physical gratification, the notion of bettering one's condition, the excitement of competition, the charm of anticipated success, are so

From Alexis de Tocqueville, *Democracy in America*, (Boston: John Allyn, 1876), Vol. II, Book I, pp. 86–93, 94–95.

many spurs to urge men onward in the active professions they have embraced, without allowing them to deviate for an instant from the track. The main stress of the faculties is to this point. The imagination is not extinct; but its chief function is to devise what may be useful, and to represent what is real. The principle of equality not only diverts men from the description of ideal beauty; it also diminishes the number of objects to be described.

Aristocracy, by maintaining society in a fixed position, is favorable to the solidity and duration of positive religions as well as to the stability of political institutions. It not only keeps the human mind within a certain sphere of belief, but it predisposes the mind to adopt one faith rather than another. An aristocratic people will always be prone to place intermediate powers between God and man. In this respect, it may be said that the aristocratic element is favorable to poetry. When the universe is peopled with supernatural beings, not palpable to sense, but discovered by the mind, the imagination ranges freely; and poets, finding a thousand subjects to delineate, also find a countless audience to take an interest in their productions.

In democratic ages it sometimes happens, on the contrary, that men are as much afloat in matters of faith as they are in their laws. Skepticism then draws the imagination of poets back to earth and confines them to the real and visible world. Even when the principle of equality does not disturb religious conviction, it tends to simplify it and to divert attention from secondary agents, to fix it principally on the Supreme Power.

Aristocracy naturally leads the human mind to the contemplation of the past and fixes it there. Democracy, on the contrary, gives men a sort of instinctive distaste for what is ancient. In this respect aristocracy is far more favorable to poetry; for things commonly grow larger and more obscure as they are more remote, and for this twofold reason they are better suited to the delineation of the ideal.

After having deprived poetry of the past, the principle of equality robs it in part of the present. Amongst aristocratic nations, there is a certain number of privileged personages, whose situation is, as it were, without and above the condition of man: to these, power, wealth, fame, wit, refinement, and distinction in all things appear peculiarly to belong. The crowd never sees them very closely, or does not watch them in minute details; and little is needed to make the description of such men poetical. On the other hand, amongst the same people you will meet with classes so ignorant, low, and enslaved that they are no less fit objects for poetry, from the excess of their rudeness and wretchedness, than the former are from their greatness and refinement. Besides, as the different classes of which an aristocratic community is composed are widely separated and imperfectly acquainted with each other, the imagination may always represent them with some addition to, or some subtraction from, what they really are.

In democratic communities, where men are all insignificant and very much alike, each man instantly sees all his fellows when he surveys himself. The poets of democratic ages can never, therefore, take any man in particular as the subject of a piece; for an object of slender importance, which is distinctly seen on all sides, will never lend itself to an ideal conception.

Thus the principle of equality, in proportion as it has established itself in the world, has dried up most of the old springs of poetry. Let us now attempt to show what new ones it may disclose.

When skepticism had depopulated heaven, and the progress of equality had reduced each individual to smaller and better-known proportions, the poets, not yet aware of what they could substitute for the great themes which were departing together with the aristocracy, turned their eyes to inanimate nature. As they lost sight of gods and heroes, they set themselves to describe streams and mountains. Thence originated, in the last century, that kind of poetry which has been called, by way of distinction, *descriptive*. Some have thought that this embellished delineation of all the physical and inanimate objects which cover the earth was the kind of poetry peculiar to democratic ages; but I believe this to be an error, and that it belongs only to a period of transition.

I am persuaded that, in the end, democracy diverts the imagination from all that is external to man, and fixes it on man alone. Democratic nations may amuse themselves for a while with considering the productions of nature; but they are excited in reality only by a survey of themselves. Here, and here alone, the true sources of poetry among such nations are to be found; and it may be believed that the poets who shall neglect to draw their inspirations hence, will lose all sway over the minds which they would enchant, and will be left in the end with none but unimpassioned spectators of their transports.

I have shown how the ideas of progression and of the indefinite perfectibility of the human race belong to democratic ages. Democratic nations care but little for what has been, but they are haunted by visions of what will be; in this direction, their unbounded imagination grows and dilates beyond all measure. Here, then, is the widest range open to the genius of poets, which allows them to remove their performances to a sufficient distance from the eye. Democracy, which shuts the past against the poet, opens the future before him.

As all the citizens who compose a democratic community are nearly equal and alike, the poet cannot dwell upon any one of them; but the nation itself invites the exercise of his powers. The general similitude of individuals, which renders any one of them taken separately an ⸻ r subject of poetry, allows poets to include them all in the same imagery, and to take a general survey of the people itself. Democratic nations have a clearer perception than any others of their own aspect; and an aspect so imposing is admirably fitted to the delineation of the ideal.

I readily admit that the Americans have no poets; I cannot allow that they have no poetic ideas. In Europe people talk a great deal of the wilds of America, but the Americans themselves never think about them: they are insensible to the wonders of inanimate nature, and they may be said not to perceive the mighty forests which surround them till they fall beneath the hatchet. Their eyes are fixed upon another sight: the American people views its own march across these wilds — drying swamps, turning the course of rivers, peopling solitudes, and subduing nature. This magnificent image of themselves does not meet the gaze of the Americans at intervals only; it may be said to haunt every one of them in his least as well as in his most important actions and to be always flitting before his mind.

Nothing conceivable is so petty, so insipid, so crowded with paltry interests, in one word, so anti-poetic, as the life of a man in the United States. But amongst the thoughts which it suggests, there is always one which is full of poetry, and this is the hidden nerve which gives vigor to the whole frame.

In aristocratic ages, each people, as well as each individual, is prone to stand separate and aloof from all others. In democratic ages, the extreme fluctuations of men, and the impatience of their desires, keep them perpetually on the move; so that the inhabitants of different countries intermingle, see, listen to, and borrow from each other. It is not only, then, the members of the same community who grow more alike; communities themselves are assimilated to one another, and the whole assemblage presents to the eye of the spectator one vast democracy, each citizen of which is a nation. This displays the aspect of mankind for the first time in the broadest light. All that belongs to the existence of the human race taken as a whole, to its vicissitudes and its future, becomes an abundant mine of poetry.

The poets who lived in aristocratic ages have been eminently successful in their delineations of certain incidents in the life of a people or a man; but none of them ever ventured to include within his performances the destinies of mankind — a task which poets writing in democratic ages may attempt.

At that same time at which every man, raising his eyes above his country, begins at length to discern mankind at large, the Deity is more and more manifest to the human mind in full and entire majesty. If, in democratic ages, faith in positive religion be often shaken, and the belief in intermediate agents, by whatever name they are called, be overcast; on the other hand men are disposed to conceive a far broader idea of Providence itself, and its interference in human affairs assumes a new and more imposing appearance to their eyes. Looking at the human race as one great whole, they easily conceive that its destinies are regulated by the same design; and in the actions of every individual they are led to acknowledge a trace of that universal and eternal plan on which God rules our race. This consideration may be taken as another prolific source of poetry which is opened in democratic times.

Democratic poets will always appear trivial and frigid if they seek to invest gods, demons, or angels with corporeal forms, and if they attempt to draw them down from heaven to dispute the supremacy of earth. But if they strive to connect the great events they commemorate with the general providential designs which govern the universe, and, without showing the finger of the Supreme Governor, reveal the thoughts of the Supreme Mind, their works will be admired and understood, for the imagination of their contemporaries takes this direction of its own accord.

It may be foreseen in like manner, that poets living in democratic times will prefer the delineation of passions and ideas to that of persons and achievements. The language, the dress, and the daily actions of men in democracies are repugnant to conceptions of the ideal. These things are not poetical in themselves; and if it were otherwise, they would cease to be so, because they are too familiar to all those to whom the poet would speak of them. This forces the poet constantly to search below the external surface which is palpable to the senses, in order to read the inner soul: and nothing lends itself more to the delineation of the ideal, than the scrutiny of the hidden depths in the immaterial nature of man. I need not traverse earth and sky to discover a wondrous object woven of contrasts, of infinite greatness and littleness, of intense gloom and amazing brightness — capable at once of exciting pity, admiration, terror, contempt. I have only to look at myself. Man springs out of nothing, crosses time, and disappears forever in the bosom of God; he is seen but for a moment, wandering on the verge of the two abysses, and there he is lost.

If man were wholly ignorant of himself, he would have no poetry in him; for it is impossible to describe what the mind does not conceive. If man clearly discerned his own nature, his imagination would remain idle, and would have nothing to add to the picture. But the nature of man is sufficiently disclosed for him to apprehend something of himself, and sufficiently obscure for all the rest to be plunged in thick darkness, in which he gropes forever — and forever in vain — to lay hold on some completer notion of his being.

Amongst a democratic people, poetry will not be fed with legends or the memorials of old traditions. The poet will not attempt to people the universe with supernatural beings, in whom his readers and his own fancy have ceased to believe; nor will he coldly personify virtues and vices, which are better received under their own features. All these resources fail him; but Man remains, and the poet needs no more. The destinies of mankind — man himself, taken aloof from his country and his age, and standing in the presence of Nature and of God, with his passions, his doubts, his rare prosperities and inconceivable wretchedness — will become the chief, if not the sole, theme of poetry among these nations.

Experience may confirm this assertion, if we consider the productions of the greatest poets who have appeared since the world has been turned to democracy. The authors of our age who have so admirably delineated the features of Faust, Childe Harold, René, and Jocelyn, did not seek to record the actions of an individual, but to enlarge and to throw light on some of the obscurer recesses of the human heart.

Such are the poems of democracy. The principle of equality does not then destroy all the subjects of poetry: it renders them less numerous, but more vast.

WHY AMERICAN WRITERS AND ORATORS OFTEN USE AN INFLATED STYLE

I have frequently remarked that the Americans, who generally treat of business in clear, plain language, devoid of all ornament, and so extremely simple as to be often coarse, are apt to become inflated as soon as they attempt a more poetical diction. They then vent their pomposity from one end of a harangue to the other; and to hear them lavish imagery on every occasion, one might fancy that they never spoke of anything with simplicity.

The English less frequently commit a similar fault. The cause of this may be pointed out without much difficulty. In democratic communities, each citizen is habitually engaged in the contemplation of a very puny object, namely, himself. If he ever raises his looks higher, he perceives only the immense form of society at large, or the still more imposing aspect of mankind. His ideas are all either extremely minute and clear, or extremely general and vague: what lies between is a void. When he has been drawn out of his own sphere, therefore, he always expects that some amazing object will be offered to his attention; and it is on these terms alone that he consents to tear himself for a moment from the petty, complicated cares which form the charm and the excitement of his life.

This appears to me sufficiently to explain why men in democracies, whose concerns are in general so paltry, call upon their poets for conceptions so vast and descriptions so unlimited.

The authors, on their part, do not fail to obey a propensity of which they themselves partake; they perpetually inflate their imaginations, and, expanding them beyond all bounds, they not unfrequently abandon the great in order to reach the gigantic. By these means, they hope to attract the observation of the multitude, and to fix it easily upon themselves: nor are their hopes disappointed; for, as the multitude seeks for nothing in poetry but objects of vast dimensions, it has neither the time to measure with accuracy the proportions of all the objects set before it, nor a taste sufficiently correct to perceive at once in what respect they are out of proportion. The author and the public at once vitiate one another.

We have also seen, that amongst democratic nations, the sources of poetry are grand, but not abundant. They are soon exhausted: and poets, not finding the elements of the ideal in what is real and true, abandon them entirely and create monsters. I do not fear that the poetry of democratic nations will prove insipid, or that it will fly too near the ground; I rather apprehend that it will be forever losing itself in the clouds, and that it will range at last to purely imaginary regions. I fear that the productions of democratic poets may often be surcharged with immense and incoherent imagery, with exaggerated descriptions and strange creations; and that the fantastic beings of their brain may sometimes make us regret the world of reality.

Walt Whitman: FROM PREFACE TO LEAVES OF GRASS (1855)

The 1855 edition of Leaves of Grass *begins with a prose essay announcing the poet's purpose. It is written in a flowing, repetitive style that heightens the prophetic tone Whitman wants. He sees himself as a kind of priest of American democracy. In the following excerpts the asterisks (* * * *) indicate deletions by the present editor.*

AMERICA does not repel the past or what it has produced under its forms or amid other politics or the idea of castes or the old religions . . . accepts the lesson with calmness . . . is not so impatient as has been supposed that the slough still sticks to opinions and manners and literature while the life which served its requirements has passed into the new life of the new forms . . . perceives that the corpse is slowly borne from the eating and sleeping rooms of the house . . . perceives that it waits a little while in the door . . . that it was fittest for its days . . . that its action has descended to the stalwart and well-shaped heir who approaches . . . and that he shall be fittest for his days.

The Americans of all nations at any time upon the earth have probably the fullest poetical nature. The United States themselves are essentially the greatest poem. In the history of the earth hitherto the largest and most stirring appear tame and orderly to their ampler largeness and stir. Here at last is something in the doings of man that corresponds with the broadcast doings of the day and night. Here is not merely a nation but a teeming nation of nations.

*　*　*

Other states indicate themselves in their deputies . . . but the genius of the United States is not best or most in its executives or legislatures, nor in its ambassadors or authors or colleges or churches or parlors, nor even in its newspapers or inventors . . . but always most in the common people. Their manners, speech, dress, friendships — the freshness and candor of their physiognomy — the picturesque looseness of their carriage . . . their deathless attachment to freedom — their aversion to anything indecorous or soft or mean — the practical acknowledgment of the citizens of one state by the citizens of all other states — the fierceness of their roused resentment — their curiosity and welcome of novelty — their self-esteem and wonderful sympathy — their susceptibility to a slight — the air they have of persons who never knew how it felt to stand in the presence of superiors — the fluency of their speech — their delight in music, the sure symptom of manly tenderness and native elegance of soul . . . their good temper and open-handedness — the terrible significance of their elections — the President's taking off his hat to them not they to him — these too are unrhymed poetry. It awaits the gigantic and generous treatment worthy of it.

The largeness of nature or the nation were monstrous without a corresponding largeness and generosity of the spirit of the citizen. Not nature nor swarming states nor streets and steamships nor prosperous business nor farms nor capital nor learning may suffice for the ideal of man . . . nor suffice the poet. No reminiscences may suffice either. A live nation can always cut a deep mark and can have the best authority the cheapest . . . namely from its own soul. This is the sum of the profitable uses of individuals or states and of present action and grandeur and of the subjects of poets. — As if it were necessary to trot back generation after generation to the eastern records! As if the beauty and sacredness of the demonstrable must fall behind that of the mythical! As if men do not make their mark out of any times! As if the opening of the western continent by discovery and what has transpired since in North and South America were less than the small theatre of the antique or the aimless sleep-walking of the middle ages! The pride of the United States leaves the wealth and finesse of the cities and all returns of commerce and agriculture and all the magnitude of geography or shows of exterior victory to enjoy the breed of fullsized men or one fullsized man unconquerable and simple.

The American poets are to enclose old and new for America is the race of races. Of them a bard is to be commensurate with a people. To him the other continents arrive as contribution . . . he gives them reception for their sake and his own sake. His spirit responds to his country's spirit . . . he incarnates its geography and natural life and rivers and lakes.

For such the expression of the American poet is to be transcendent and new. It is to be indirect and not direct or descriptive or epic. Its quality goes through these to much more. Let the age and wars of other nations be chanted and their eras and characters be illustrated and that finish the verse. Not so the great psalm of the republic. Here the theme is creative and has vista. Here comes one among the wellbeloved stonecutters and plans with decision and science and sees the solid and beautiful forms of the future where there are now no solid forms.

Of all nations the United States with veins full of poetical stuff most need poets and will doubtless have the greatest and use them the greatest. Their Presidents shall not be their common referee so much as their poets shall. Of all mankind the great poet is the equable man. Not in him but off from him things are grotesque or eccentric or fail of their sanity. Nothing out of its place is good and nothing in its place is bad. He bestows on every object or quality its fit proportions neither more nor less. He is the arbiter of the diverse and he is the key. He is the equalizer of his age and land . . . he supplies what wants supplying and checks what wants checking.

*   *   *

The greatest poet hardly knows pettiness or triviality. If he breathes into any thing that was before thought small it dilates with the grandeur and life of the universe. He is a seer . . . he is individual . . . he is complete in himself . . . the others are as good as he, only he sees it and they do not. He is not one of the chorus . . . he does not stop for any regulation . . . he is the president of regulation. What the eyesight does to the rest he does to the rest. Who knows the curious mystery of the eyesight? The other senses corroborate themselves, but this is removed from any proof but its own and foreruns the identities of the spiritual world. A single glance of it mocks all the investigations of man and all the instruments and books of the earth and all reasoning. What is marvellous? what is unlikely? what is impossible or baseless or vague? after you have once just opened the space of a peachpit and given audience to far and near and to the sunset and had all things enter with electric swiftness softly and duly without confusion or jostling or jam.

The land and sea, the animals, fishes and birds, the sky of heaven and the orbs, the forests mountains and rivers, are not small themes . . . but folks expect of the poet to indicate more than the beauty and dignity which always attach to dumb real objects . . . they expect him to indicate the path between reality and their souls. Men and women perceive the beauty well enough . . . probably as well as he. The passionate tenacity of hunters, woodmen, early risers, cultivators of gardens and orchards and fields, the love of healthy women for the manly form, seafaring persons, drivers of horses, the passion for light and the open air, all is an old varied sign of the unfailing perception of beauty and of a residence of the poetic in outdoor people. They can never be assisted by poets to perceive . . . some may but they never can. The poetic quality is not marshalled in rhyme or uniformity or abstract addresses to things nor in melancholy complaints or good precepts, but is the life of these and much else and is in the soul. The profit of rhyme is that it drops seeds of a sweeter and more luxuriant rhyme, and of uniformity that it conveys itself into its own roots in the ground out of sight. The rhyme and uniformity of perfect poems show the free growth of metrical laws and bud from them as unerringly and loosely as lilacs or roses on a bush, and take shapes as compact as the shapes of chestnuts and oranges and melons and pears, and shed the perfume impalpable to form. The fluency and ornaments of the finest poems or music or orations or recitations are not independent but dependent.

*   *   *

The fruition of beauty is no chance of hit or miss . . . it is inevitable as life . . . it is exact and plumb as gravitation. From the eyesight proceeds another eyesight and from the hearing proceeds another hearing and from the voice proceeds another voice eternally curious of the harmony of things with man. To these respond perfections not only in the committees that were supposed to stand for the rest but in the rest themselves just the same. These understand the law of perfection in masses and floods . . . that its finish is to each for itself and onward from itself . . . that it is profuse and impartial . . . that there is not a minute of the light or dark nor an acre of the earth or sea without it — nor any direction of the sky nor any trade or employment nor, any turn of events. This is the reason that about the proper expression of beauty there is precision and balance . . . one part does not need to be thrust above another. The best singer is not the one who has the most lithe and powerful organ . . . the pleasure of poems is not in them that take the handsomest measure and similes and sound.

*   *   *

The art of art, the glory of expression and the sunshine of the light of letters is simplicity. Nothing is better than simplicity . . . nothing can make up for

excess or for the lack of definiteness. To carry on the heave of impulse and pierce intellectual depths and give all subjects their articulations are powers neither common nor very uncommon. But to speak in literature with the perfect rectitude and insouciance of the movements of animals and the unimpeachableness of the sentiment of trees in the woods and grass by the roadside is the flawless triumph of art. If you have looked on him who has achieved it you have looked on one of the masters of the artists of all nations and times. You shall not contemplate the flight of the graygull over the bay or the mettlesome action of the blood horse or the tall leaning of sunflowers on their stalk or the appearance of the sun journeying through heaven or the appearance of the moon afterward with any more satisfaction than you shall contemplate him. The greatest poet has less a marked style and is more the channel of thoughts and things without increase or diminution, and is the free channel of himself. He swears to his art, I will not be meddlesome, I will not have in my writing any elegance or effect or originality to hang in the way between me and the rest like curtains. I will have nothing hang in the way, not the richest curtains. What I tell I tell for precisely what it is. Let who may exalt or startle or fascinate or soothe; I will have purposes as health or heat or snow has and be as regardless of observation. What I experience or portray shall go from my composition without a shred of my composition. You shall stand by my side and look in the mirror with me.

The old red blood and stainless gentility of great poets will be proved by their unconstraint. A heroic person walks at his ease through and out of that custom or precedent or authority that suits him not. Of the traits of the brotherhood of writers savants musicians inventors and artists nothing is finer than silent defiance advancing from new free forms. In the need of poems philosophy politics mechanism science behaviour, the craft of art, an appropriate native grand-opera, shipcraft, or any craft, he is greatest forever and forever who contributes the greatest original practical example. The cleanest expression is that which finds no sphere worthy of itself and makes one.

The messages of great poets to each man and woman are, Come to us on equal terms, Only then can you understand us, We are no better than you, What we enclose you enclose, What we enjoy you may enjoy. Did you suppose there could be only one Supreme? We affirm there can be unnumbered Supremes, and that one does not countervail another any more than one eyesight countervails another . . . and that men can be good or grand only of the consciousness of their supremacy within them. What do you think is the grandeur of storms and dismemberments and the deadliest battles and wrecks and the wildest fury of the elements and the power of the sea and the motion of nature and of the throes of human desires and dignity and hate and love? It is that something in the soul which says, Rage on, Whirl on, I tread master here and everywhere, Master of the spasms of the sky and of the shatter of the sea, Master of nature and passion and death, And of all terror and all pain.

The American bards shall be marked for generosity and affection and for encouraging competitors . . . They shall be kosmos . . . without monopoly or secresy . . . glad to pass any thing to any one . . . hungry for equals night and day. They shall not be careful of riches and privilege . . . they shall be riches and privilege . . . they shall perceive who the most affluent man is. The most affluent man is he that confronts all the shows he sees by equivalents out of the stronger wealth of himself. The American bard shall delineate no class of persons nor one or two out of the strata of interests nor love most nor truth most nor the soul most nor the body most . . . and not be for the eastern states more than the western or the northern states more than the southern.

Exact science and its practical movements are no checks on the greatest poet but always his encouragement and support. The outset and remembrance are there . . . there the arms that lifted him first and brace him best . . . there he returns after all his goings and comings. The sailor and traveler . . . the anatomist chemist astronomer geologist phrenologist spiritualist mathematician historian and lexicographer are not poets, but they are the lawgivers of poets and their construction underlies the structure of every perfect poem. No matter what rises or is uttered they sent the seed of the conception of it . . . of them and by them stand the visible proofs of souls . . . always of their fatherstuff must be begotten the sinewy races of bards. If there shall be love and content between the father and the son and if the greatness of the son is the exuding of the greatness of the father there shall be love between the poet and the man of demonstrable science. In the beauty of poems are the tuft and final applause of science.

Great is the faith of the flush of knowledge and of the investigation of the depths of qualities and things. Cleaving and circling here swells the soul of the poet yet is president of itself always. The depths are fathomless and therefore calm. The innocence and nakedness are resumed . . . they are neither modest nor immodest. The whole theory of the special and supernatural and all that was twined with it or educed out of it departs as a dream. What has ever happened . . . what happens and whatever may or shall happen, the vital laws enclose all . . . they are sufficient for any case and for all cases . . . none to be hurried or retarded . . . any miracle of affairs or persons inadmissible in the vast clear scheme where every motion and every spear of grass and the frames and spirits of men and women and all that concerns them are unspeakably perfect miracles all referring to all and each distinct and in its place. It is also not consistent with the reality of the soul to admit that there is anything in the known universe more divine than men and women.

Men and women and the earth and all upon it are simply to be taken as they are, and the investigation of their past and present and future shall be unintermitted and shall be done with perfect candor. Upon this basis philosophy speculates ever looking toward the poet, ever regarding the eternal tendencies of all toward happiness never inconsistent with what is clear to the senses and to the soul. For the eternal tendencies of all toward happiness make the only point of sane philosophy. Whatever comprehends less than that . . . whatever is less than the laws of light and of astronomical motion . . . or less than the laws that follow the thief the liar the glutton and the drunkard through this life and doubtless afterward . . . or less than vast stretches of time or the slow formation of density or the patient upheaving of strata — is of no account. Whatever would put God in a poem or system of philosophy as contending against some being or influence is also of no account. Sanity and ensemble characterise the great master . . . spoilt in one principle all is spoilt. The great master has nothing

to do with miracles. He sees health for himself in being one of the mass . . . he sees the hiatus in singular eminence. To the perfect shape comes common ground. To be under the general law is great for that is to correspond with it. The master knows that he is unspeakably great and that all are unspeakably great . . . that nothing for instance is greater than to conceive children and bring them up well . . . that to be is just as great as to perceive or tell.

In the make of the great masters the idea of political liberty is indispensable. Liberty takes the adherence of heroes wherever men and women exist . . . but never takes any adherence or welcome from the rest more than from poets. They are the voice and exposition of liberty. They out of ages are worthy the grand idea . . . to them it is confided and they must sustain it. Nothing has precedence of it and nothing can warp or degrade it. The attitude of great poets is to cheer up slaves and horrify despots. The turn of their necks, the sound of their feet, the motions of their wrists, are full of hazard to the one and hope to the other. Come nigh them awhile and though they neither speak or advise you shall learn the faithful American lesson. Liberty is poorly served by men whose good intent is quelled from one failure or two failures or any number of failures, or from the casual indifference or ingratitude of the people, or from the sharp show of the tushes of power, or the bringing to bear soldiers and cannon or any penal statutes. Liberty relies upon itself, invites no one, promises nothing, sits in calmness and light, is positive and composed, and knows no discouragement. The battle rages with many a loud alarm and frequent advance and retreat . . . the enemy triumphs . . . the prison, the handcuffs, the iron necklace and anklet, the scaffold, garrote and leadballs do their work . . . the cause is asleep . . . the strong throats are choked with their own blood . . . the young men drop their eyelashes toward the ground when they pass each other . . . and is liberty gone out of that place? No never. When liberty goes it is not the first to go nor the second or third to go . . . it waits for all the rest to go . . . it is the last . . . When the memories of the old martyrs are faded utterly away . . . when the large names of patriots are laughed at in the public halls from the lips of the orators . . . when the boys are no more christened after the same but christened after tyrants and traitors instead . . . when the laws of the free are grudgingly permitted and laws for informers and bloodmoney are sweet to the taste of the people . . . when I and you walk abroad upon the earth stung with compassion at the sight of numberless brothers answering our equal friendship and calling no man master — and when we are elated with noble joy at the sight of slaves . . . when the soul retires in the cool communion of the night and surveys its experience and has much extasy over the word and deed that put back a helpless innocent person into the gripe of the gripers or into any cruel inferiority . . . when those in all parts of these states who could easier realize the true American character but do not yet — when the swarms of cringers, suckers, doughfaces, lice of politics, planners of sly involutions for their own preferment to city officers or state legislatures or the judiciary or congress or the presidency, obtain a response of love and natural deference from the people whether they get the offices or no . . . when it is better to be a bound booby and rogue in office at a high salary than the poorest free mechanic or farmer with his hat unmoved from his head and firm eyes and a candid and generous heart . . . and when servility by town or state or the federal government or any oppression on a large scale or small scale can be tried on without its own punishment following duly after in exact proportion against the smallest chance of escape . . . or rather when all life and all the souls of men and women are discharged from any part of the earth — then only shall the instinct of liberty be discharged from that part of the earth.

As the attributes of the poets of the kosmos concentre in the real body and soul and in the pleasure of things they possess the superiority of genuineness over all fiction and romance. As they emit themselves facts are showered over with light . . . the daylight is lit with more volatile light . . . also the deep between the setting and rising sun goes deeper many fold. Each precise object or condition or combination or process exhibits a beauty . . . the multiplication table its — old age its — the carpenter's trade its — the grandopera its . . . the hugehulled cleanshaped New-York clipper at sea under steam or full sail gleams with unmatched beauty . . . the American circles and large harmonies of government gleam with theirs . . . and the commonest definite intentions and actions with theirs. The poets of the kosmos advance through all interpositions and coverings and turmoils and stratagems to first principles. They are of use . . . they dissolve poverty from its need and riches from its conceit. You large proprietor they say shall not realize or perceive more than any one else. The owner of the library is not he who holds a legal title to it having bought and paid for it. Any one and every one is owner of the library who can read the same through all the varieties of tongues and subjects and styles, and in whom they enter with ease and take residence and force toward paternity and maternity, and make supple and powerful and rich and large. . . . These American states strong and healthy and accomplished shall receive no pleasure from violations of natural models and must not permit them. In paintings or mouldings or carvings in mineral or wood, or in the illustrations of books or newspapers, or in any comic or tragic prints, or in the patterns of woven stuffs or any thing to beautify rooms or furniture or costumes, or to put upon cornices or monuments or on the prows or sterns of ships, or to put anywhere before the human eye indoors or out, that which distorts honest shapes or which creates unearthly beings or places or contingencies is a nuisance and revolt. Of the human form especially it is so great it must never be made ridiculous. Of ornaments to a work nothing outre can be allowed . . . but those ornaments can be allowed that conform to the perfect facts of the open air and that flow out of the nature of the work and come irrepressibly from it and are necessary to the completion of the work. Most works are most beautiful without ornament . . . Exaggerations will be revenged in human physiology. Clean and vigorous children are jetted and conceived only in those communities where the models of natural forms are public every day. . . . Great genius and the people of these states must never be demeaned to romances. As soon as histories are properly told there is no more need of romances.

*   *   *

The direct trial of him who would be the greatest poet is today. If he does not flood himself with the immediate age as with vast oceanic tides . . . and if he does not attract his own land body and soul to himself and hang on its neck with incomparable love and plunge his semitic muscle into its merits and demerits . . . and if he be not himself the age transfigured . . . and if to him is not opened the eternity which gives similitude to all periods and locations and processes and animate and inanimate forms, and which is the bond of time, and rises up from its inconceivable vagueness and infiniteness in the swimming shape of today, and is held by the ductile anchors of life, and makes the present spot the passage from what was to what shall be, and commits itself to the representation of this wave of an hour and this one of the sixty beautiful children of the wave — let him merge in the general run and wait his development . . . Still the final test of poems or any character or work remains. The prescient poet projects himself centuries ahead and judges performer or performance after the changes of time. Does it live through them? Does it still hold on untired? Will the same style and the direction of genius to similar points be satisfactory now? Has no new discovery in science or arrival at superior planes of thought and judgment and behavior fixed him or his so that either can be looked down upon? Have the marches of tens and hundreds and thousands of years made willing detours to the right hand and the left hand for his sake? Is he beloved long and long after he is buried? Does the young man think often of him? and the young woman think often of him? and do the middle-aged and the old think of him?

A great poem is for ages and ages in common and for all degrees and complexions and all departments and sects and for a woman as much as a man and a man as much as a woman. A great poem is no finish to a man or woman but rather a beginning. Has any one fancied he could sit at last under some due authority and rest satisfied with explanations and realize and be content and full? To no such terminus does the greatest poet bring . . . he brings neither cessation or sheltered fatness and ease. The touch of him tells in action. Whom he takes he takes with firm sure grasp into live regions previously unattained . . . thenceforward is no rest . . . they see the space and ineffable sheen that turn the old spots and lights into dead vacuums. The companion of him beholds the birth and progress of stars and learns one of the meanings. Now there shall be a man cohered out of tumult and chaos . . . the elder encourages the younger and shows him how . . . they two shall launch off fearlessly together till the new world fits an orbit for itself and looks unabashed on the lesser orbits of the stars and sweeps through the ceaseless rings and shall never be quiet again.

There will soon be no more priests. Their work is done. They may wait a while . . . perhaps a generation or two. . . dropping off by degrees. A superior breed shall take their place . . . the gangs of kosmos and prophets en masse shall take their place. A new order shall arise and they shall be the priests of man, and every man shall be his own priest. The churches built under their umbrage shall be the churches of men and women. Through the divinity of themselves shall the kosmos and the new breed of poets be interpreters of men and women and of all events and things. They shall find their inspiration in real objects today, symptoms of the past and future. . . . They shall not deign to defend immortality or God or the perfection of things or liberty or the exquisite beauty and reality of the soul. They shall arise in America and be responded to from the remainder of the earth.

The English language befriends the grand American expression . . . it is brawny enough and limber and full enough. On the tough stock of a race who through all change of circumstance was never without the idea of political liberty, which is the animus of all liberty, it has attracted the terms of daintier and gayer and subtler and more elegant tongues. It is the powerful language of resistance . . . it is the dialect of common sense. It is the speech of the proud and melancholy races and of all who aspire. It is the chosen tongue to express growth faith self-esteem freedom justice equality friendliness amplitude prudence decision and courage. It is the medium that shall well nigh express the inexpressible.

No great literature nor any like style of behaviour or oratory or social intercourse or household arrangements or public institutions or the treatment by bosses of employed people, nor executive detail or detail of the army or navy, nor spirit of legislation or courts or police or tuition or architecture or songs or amusements or the costumes of young men, can long elude the jealous and passionate instinct of American standards. Whether or no the sign appears from the mouths of the people, it throbs a live interrogation in every freeman's and freewoman's heart after that which passes by or this built to remain. Is it uniform with my country? Are its disposals without ignominious distinctions? Is it for the ever-growing communes of brothers and lovers, large, well-united, proud beyond the old models, generous beyond all models? Is it something grown fresh out of the fields or drawn from the sea for use to me today here? I know that what answers for me an American must answer for any individual or nation that serves for a part of my materials. Does this answer? or is it without reference to universal needs? or sprung of the needs of the less developed society of special ranks? or old needs of pleasure overlaid by modern science and forms? Does this acknowledge liberty with audible and absolute acknowledgement, and set slavery at nought for life and death? Will it help breed one good-shaped and well-hung man, and a woman to be his perfect and independent mate? Does it improve manners? Is it for the nursing of the young of the republic? Does it solve readily with the sweet milk of the nipples of the breasts of the mother of many children? Has it too the old ever-fresh forbearance and impartiality? Does it look with the same love on the last born and on those hardening toward stature, and on the errant, and on those who disdain all strength of assault outside of their own?

The poems distilled from other poems will probably pass away. The coward will surely pass away. The expectation of the vital and great can only be satisfied by the demeanor of the vital and great. The swarms of the polished depre-cating and reflectors and the polite float off and leave no remembrance. America prepares with composure and goodwill for the visitors that have sent word. It is not intellect that is to be their warrant and welcome. The talented, the artist, the ingenious, the editor, the statesman, the erudite . . . they are not unappreciated . . . they fall in their place and do their work. The soul of the nation also does its work No disguise can pass on it . . . no disguise can conceal from it. It rejects none, it permits all. Only toward as good as itself and toward the like of itself will it advance half-way. An individual is as superb as a nation when he has the qualities which make a superb nation. The soul of the largest and wealthiest and proudest nation may well go half-way to meet that of its poets. The signs are effectual. There is no fear of mistake. If the one is true the other is true. The proof of a poet is that his country absorbs him as affectionately as he has absorbed it.

Edward Dowden: THE POETRY OF DEMOCRACY

"God save us from Whitmanism," wrote the editor of an English review in rejecting this essay by Edward Dowden (1843–1913). Dowden was a distinguished Shakespearean scholar and Professor of English Literature at Trinity College, Dublin. After several other rejections, his essay finally appeared in the Westminster Review *in 1871. By that time Whitman had a number of enthusiastic admirers in England (probably more than in America), among them: William Michael Rossetti, John Symonds, Moncure Conway, and Algernon Charles Swinburne. In the present volume Dowden speaks for Whitman's earliest European audience.*

AT last steps forward a man unlike any of his predecessors, and announces himself, and is announced with a flourish of critical trumpets, as Bard of America, and Bard of democracy. What cannot be questioned after an hour's acquaintance

From *Studies in Literature, 1789–1877*, (London, 1892), pp. 473–496. The essay is slightly abridged for the present edition.

with Walt Whitman and his "Leaves of Grass," is that in him we meet a man not shaped out of old-world clay, not cast in any old-world mould, and hard to name by any old-world name. In his self-assertion there is a manner of powerful nonchalantness which is not assumed; he does not peep timidly from behind his works to glean our suffrages, but seems to say, "Take me or leave me, here I am, a solid and not an inconsiderable fact of the universe." He disturbs our classifications. He attracts us; he repels us; he excites our curiosity, wonder, admiration, love; or, our extreme repugnance. He does anything except leave us indifferent. However we feel towards him we cannot despise him. He is "a summons and a challenge." He must be understood and so accepted, or must be got rid of. Passed by he cannot be. His critics have, for the most part, confined their attention to the personality of the man; they have studied him, for the most part, as a phenomenon isolated from the surrounding society, the environment, the *milieu,* which has made such a phenomenon possible. In a general way it has been said that Whitman is the representative in art of American democracy, but the meaning of this has not been investigated in detail. It is purposed here to consider some of the characteristics of democratic art, and to inquire in what manner they manifest themselves in Whitman's work.

A word of explanation is necessary. The representative man of a nation is not always the nation's favourite. Hebrew spiritualism, the deepest instincts, the highest reaches of the moral attainment of the Jewish race, appear in the cryings and communings of its prophets; yet the prophets sometimes cried in the wilderness, and the people went after strange gods. American democracy is as yet but half-formed. The framework of its institutions exists, but the will, the conscience, the mature desires of the democratic society are still in process of formation. If Whitman's writings are spoken of as the poetry of American democracy, it is not implied that his are the volumes most inquired after in the libraries of New York or Boston. What we mean is that these are the poems which naturally arise when a man of imaginative genius stands face to face with a great democratic world, as yet but half-fashioned, such as society is in the United States of the present day. Successive editions of his works prove that Whitman has many readers. But whether he had them now, or waited for them in years to come, it would remain true that he is the first representative democrat in art of the American continent. Not that he is to be regarded as a model or a guide; great principles and great passions which must play their part in the future, are to be found in his writings; but these have not yet cleared themselves from their amorphous surroundings. At the same time he is before all else a living man, and must not be compelled to appear as mere official representative of anything. He will not be comprehended in a formula. No *view* of him can image the substance, the life and movement of his manhood, which contracts and dilates, and is all over sensitive and vital. Such views are, however, valuable in the study of literature, as hypotheses are in the natural sciences, at least for the colligation of facts. They have a tendency to render criticism rigid and doctrinaire; the critic must therefore ever be ready to escape from his own theory of a man, and come in contact with the man himself. Every one doubtless moves in some regular orbit, and all aberrations are only apparent, but what the precise orbit is we must be slow to pronounce. Meanwhile we may legitimately conjecture, as Kepler conjectured, if only we remain ready, as Kepler was, to vary our conjectures as the exigencies of the observed phenomena require.

A glance at the art of an aristocratic period will inform us in the way of contrast of much that we may expect to find under a democracy. And before all else we are impressed by the great regard which the artists of an aristocratic period pay to form. The dignity of letters maintains itself, like the dignity of the court, by a regulated propriety of manners. Ideas and feelings cannot be received unless they wear the courtly costume. Precise canons applicable to the drama, the ode, the epic, to painting, sculpture, architecture, music, are agreed upon, and are strictly enforced. They acquire traditional authority, the precedents of a great period of art (such, for example, as that of Louis XIV), being final and absolute with succeeding generations. "Style is deemed of almost as much importance as thought. . . . The tone of mind is always dignified, seldom very animated, and writers care more to perfect what they produce than to multiply their productions."* The peril to which an aristocratic literature is hereby exposed is of a singular kind; matter or substance may cease to exist, while an empty and elaborately studied form, a variegated surface with nothing below it, may remain. This condition of things was actually realized at different times in the literatures of Italy, of Spain, of France, and of England, when such a variegated surface of literature served for disport and display of the wits of courtiers, of ingenious authors, of noble

and gentle persons male and female, and when reflection and imagination had ceased to have any relation with letters.

Again, the literature of an aristocracy is distinguished by its striving after selectness, by its exclusive spirit, and the number of things it proscribes. This is especially the case with the courtly art which has a great monarchy for its centre of inspiration. There is an ever-present terror of vulgarity. Certain words are ineligible in poetry; they are mean or undignified, and the things denoted by them must be described in an elegant periphrasis. Directness and vividness are sacrificed to propriety. The acquired associations of words are felt to be as important, and claim as much attention as their immediate significance, their spiritual power and personal character. In language as in life there is, so to speak, an aristocracy and a commonalty; words with a heritage of dignity, words which have been ennobled, and a rabble of words which are excluded from positions of honour and of trust. But this striving after selectness in forms of speech is the least important manifestation of the exclusive spirit of aristocratic art. Far the greater number of men and women, classes of society, conditions of life, modes of thought and feeling, are not even conceived as in any way susceptible of representation in art which aspires to be grave and beautiful. The common people do not show themselves *en masse* except as they may follow in a patient herd, or oppose in impotent and insolent revolt the leadership of their lords. Individually they are never objects of equal interest with persons of elevated worldly station. Even Shakespeare could hardly find in humble life other virtues than a humorous honesty and an affectionate fidelity. Robin Hood, the popular hero, could not be quite heroic were he not

* "Democracy in America," vol. iii, p. 115, ed. 1840.

of noble extraction, and reputed Earl of Huntingdon.

In the decline of an aristocratic period, dramatic studies of individual character and the life of the peasant or artisan may be made *from a superior point of view.* The literature of benevolence and piety stooping down to view the sad bodies and souls of men tends in this direction. And there are poems and novels, and paintings and sculptures, which flatter the feeling of mild benevolence. Pictures like those of Faed, in which some aged cottager, some strong delver of the earth, or searcher of the sea, some hard-worked father of children, says appealingly, "By virtue of this love I exhibit towards my offspring, by virtue of the correct sense I have of the condescension of my betters, by virtue of this bit of pathos — indubitably human — in my eye, confess now *am* I not a man and a brother?" — pictures like these are produced, and may be purchased by amiable persons of the upper classes who would honour the admirable qualities which exist in humble life. But when the aristocratic period is in its strength, and especially in courtly art and literature, these condescending studies, not without a certain affection and sincerity in them, are unknown. It is as if the world were made up of none but the gently born and bred. At most rustic life is glanced at for the sake of the suggestions of pretty waywardness it may supply to the fancy of great people tired of greatness. . . .

Now in all these particulars the art of a democratic age exhibits characteristics precisely opposite to those of the art of an aristocracy. Form and style modelled on traditional examples are little valued. No canons of composition are agreed upon or observed without formal agreement. No critical dictator enacts laws which are accepted without dispute, and acquire additional authority during many years. Each new generation, with its new heave of life, its multitudinous energies, ideas, passions, is a law to itself. Except public opinion, there is no authority on earth above the authority of a man's own soul, and public opinion being strongly in favour of individualism, a writer is tempted to depreciate unduly the worth of order, propriety, regularity of the academic kind; he is encouraged to make new literary experiments as others make new experiments in religion; he is permitted to be true to his own instincts, whether they are beautiful instincts or the reverse. The appeal which a work of art makes is to the nation, not to a class, and diversities of style are consequently admissible. Every style can be tolerated except the vapid, everything can be accepted but that which fails to stimulate the intellect or the passions.

Turning to Whitman, we perceive at once that his work corresponds with this state of things. If he had written in England in the period of Queen Anne, if he had written in France in the period of the *grand monarque,* he must have either acknowledged the supremacy of authority in literature and submitted to it, or on the other hand revolted against it. As it is, he is remote from authority, and neither submits nor revolts. Whether we call what he has written verse or prose, we have no hesitation in saying that it is no copy, that it is something uncontrolled by any model or canon, something which takes whatever shape it possesses directly from the soul of its maker. With the Bible, Homer, and Shakespeare familiar to him Whitman writes in the presence of great models, and some influences from each have doubtless entered into his nature; but that they should possess authority over him any more than that he should possess authority over them, does not occur to him as possible. The relation of democracy to the Past comes out very notably here. Entirely assured of its own right to the Present, it is prepared to acknowledge fully the right of past generations to the Past. It is not hostile to that Past, rather claims kinship with it, but also claims equality, as a full-grown son with a father:

I conn'd old times;
I sat studying at the feet of the great masters:
Now, if eligible, O that the great masters
    might return and study me!
In the name of These States, shall I scorn
    the antique?
Why These are the children of the antique,
    to justify it.

Dead poets, philosophs, priests,
Martyrs, artists, inventors, governments long
    since,
Language-shapers on other shores,
Nations once powerful, now reduced, with-
    drawn or desolate,
I dare not proceed till I respectfully credit
    what you have left, wafted hither:
I have perused it, own it is admirable (mov-
    ing awhile among it);
Think nothing can ever be greater, — nothing
    can ever deserve more than it deserves;
Regarding it all intently a long while, — then
    dismissing it,
I stand in my place, with my own day, here.

. . . As in all else, so with regard to the form of what he writes, Walt Whitman can find no authority superior to himself, or rather to the rights of the subject which engages him. There is, as Mr. Rossetti has observed, "a very powerful and majestic rhythmical sense" throughout his writings, prose and verse (if we consent to apply the term *verse* to any of them), and this rhythmical sense, as with every great poet, is original and inborn. His works, it may be, exhibit no perfect crystal of artistic form, but each is a menstruum saturated with form in solution. He fears to lose the instinctive in any process of elaboration, the vital in anything which looks like mechanism. He does not write with a full consciousness of the processes of creation, nor does any true poet. Certain combinations of sound are preconceived, and his imagination excited by them works towards them by a kind of reflex action, automatically. His *ars poetica* is embodied in the precept that the poet should hold himself passive in presence of the material universe, in presence of society, in presence of his own soul, and become the blind yet unerringly guided force through which these seek artistic expression. No afterthought, no intrusion of reasoning, no calculating of effects, no stepping back to view his work is tolerated. The artist must create his art with as little hesitation, as little questioning of processes, and as much sureness of result as the beaver builds his house. Very nobly Whitman has spoken on this subject, and let those who, because they do not know him, suppose him insensible to any attractions in art except those of the extravagant, the incoherent, and the lawless, read what follows from the preface to "Leaves of Grass": . . .

Seeing much of deep truth in this, [a statement in the Preface about the poet as "free channel of himself"] it must be added that, when the poet broods over his half-formed creation, and fashions it with divine ingenuity, and gives it shapeliness and completion of detail, and the lustre of finished workmanship, he does not forsake his instincts, but is obedient to them; he does not remove from nature into a laboratory of art, but is the close companion of nature. The vital spontaneous movement of the faculties, far from ceasing, still goes on like "the flight of the grey-gull over the bay," while the poet seeks after order, proportion, comeliness, melody — in a word, beauty; or rather, as Whitman himself is fond of saying, does not seek but is sought — the perfect form preconceived but unattained, drawing the artist towards itself with an invincible attraction. An artist who does not yield to the desire for perfect order and beauty of form, instead of coming closer to nature is really forsaking nature, and doing violence to a genuine artistic instinct. Walt Whitman, however, knows this in all probability well enough, and does not need to be taught the mysteries of his craft. We will not say that his poems, as regards their forms, do not, after all, come right, or that for the matter which he handles his manner of treatment may not be the best possible. One feels, as it has been well said, that although no counting of syllables will reveal the mechanism of the music, the music is there, and that "one would not for something change ears with those who cannot hear it." . . .

The principle of equality upon which the democratic form of society is founded, obviously opposes itself to the exclusive spirit of the aristocratical polity. The essential thing which gives one the freedom of the world is not to be born a man of this or that rank, or class, or caste, but simply to be born a man. The literature of an aristocratic period is distinguished by its aim at selectness, and the number of things it proscribes; we should expect the literature of a democracy to be remarkable for its comprehensiveness, its acceptance of the persons of all men, its multiform sympathies. The difference between the President and the Broadway mason or hodman is inconsiderable — an accident

of office; what is common to both is the inexpressibly important thing, their inalienable humanity. Rich and poor, high and low, powerful and feeble, healthy and diseased, deformed and beautiful, old and young, man and woman, have this in common, and by possession of this are in the one essential thing equal, and brethren one of another. Even between the virtuous man and the vicious the difference is less than the agreement; they differ by a quality, but agree by the substance of their manhood. The *man* in all men, however it may be obscured by cruel shocks and wrenches of life which distort, by long unnatural uses which deform, by ignorance, by the well-meaning stupidity of others, or by one's own stupidity, by foul living, or by clean, hard, worldly living, is surely somewhere discoverable. How can any human creature be rejected, any scorned, any mocked? Such satire and such comedy as appear in aristocratic society are discouraged by the genius of democracy. The spirit of exclusiveness will, it is true, never fail to find material for its support, and baser prides may replace the calm, conservative, but unaggressive pride of hereditary dignity. Nevertheless it remains no less true that the spectacle of a great democracy present to the imagination, and the temper of the democracy accepted by the understanding heart, favour only such prides as are founded on nature — that is, on the possession, acquired or inherited, of personal qualities, personal powers, and virtues, and attainments.

If this be a true account of some characteristics of the art which arises when a man of imaginative genius stands face to face with a great democracy, Walt Whitman in these particulars is what he claims to be, a representative democrat in art. No human being is rejected by him, no one slighted, nor would he judge any, except as "the light falling around a helpless thing" judges. No one in his poems comes appealing "Am I not interesting, am I not deserving, am I not a man and a brother?" We have had, he thinks, "ducking and deprecating about enough." The poet studies no one from a superior point of view. He delights in men, and neither approaches deferentially those who are above him, nor condescendingly gazes upon those who are beneath. He is the comrade of every man, high and low. His admiration of a strong, healthy, and beautiful body, or a strong, healthy, and beautiful soul, is great when he sees it in a statesman or a savant; it is precisely as great when he sees it in the ploughman or the smith. Every variety of race and nation, every condition in society, every degree of culture, every season of human life, is accepted by Whitman as admirable and best, each in its own place. Working men of every name — all who engage in field-work, all who toil upon the sea, the city artisan, the woodsman and the trapper, fill him with pleasure by their presence; and that they are interesting to him not in a general way of theory or doctrine (a piece of the abstract democratic creed), but in the way of close, vital human sympathy, appears from the power he possesses of bringing before us with strange precision, vividness, and nearness in a few decisive strokes the essential characteristics of their respective modes of living. If the strong, full-grown working man wants a lover and comrade, he will think Walt Whitman especially made for him. If the young man wants one, he will think him especially the poet of young men. Yet a rarer and finer spell than that of the lusty vitality of youth, or the trained activity of manhood, is exercised over the poet by the beautiful repose or unsubdued energy of old age. He is "the caresser of life, wherever moving." He does not search antiquity for heroic men and beautiful women; his own abundant vitality makes all the life which surrounds him a source of completest joy; "what is commonest, cheapest, nearest, easiest, is Me . . . not asking the sky to come down to my good-will; scattering it freely for ever."

But it is not those alone who are beautiful and healthy and good who claim the poet's love. To all "the others are down on" Whitman's hand is outstretched in help, and through him come to us the voices — petitions or demands — of the diseased and despairing, of slaves, of prostitutes, of thieves, of deformed persons, of drunkards. Every man is a divine miracle to him, and he sees a *redeemer*, whom Christ will not be ashamed to acknowledge a comrade, in every one who performs an act of loving self-sacrifice:

Three scythes at harvest whizzing in a row, from three lusty angels with shirts bagged out at their waists;
The snag-tooth'd hostler with red hair redeeming sins past and to come,
Selling all he possesses, travelling on foot to fee lawyers for his brother, and sit by him while he is tried for forgery.

Does no limit, then, exist to the poet's acceptance of the persons of men? There is one test of his tolerance more severe than can be offered by the vicious or the deformed. Can he tolerate the man of science? Yes, though he were to find him peeping and botanizing upon his mother's grave. Science and democracy appear before Whitman as twin powers which bend over the modern world hand in hand, great and beneficent. Democracy seems to him that form of society which alone is scientifically justifiable; founded upon a recognition of the facts of nature, and a resolute denial of social fables, superstitions, and uninvestigated tradition. Moreover he looks to science for important elements which shall contribute to a new conception of nature and of man, and of their mutual relations, to be itself the ideal basis of a new poetry and art — "after the chemist, geologist, ethnologist, finally shall come the Poet worthy that name; the true Son of God shall come singing his songs." Lastly, Whitman has a peculiar reason of his own for loving science; he is a mystic, and such a mystic as finds positive science not unacceptable. Whitman beholds no visions of visible things in heaven or hell unseen to other men. He rather sees with extraordinary precision the realities of our earth, but he sees them, in his mystical mood, as symbols of the impalpable and spiritual. They are hieroglyphs most clear-cut, most brilliantly and definitely coloured to his eyes, but still expressive of something unseen. His own personality as far as he can give it expression or is conscious of it — that identity of himself, which is the hardest of all facts and the only entrance to all facts, is yet no more than the image projected by another ego, the real *Me*, which stands "untouched, untold, altogether unreached":

Withdrawn far, mocking me with mock-congratulatory signs and bows,
With peals of ironical laughter at every word I have written,

     ❋   ❋   ❋

Now I perceive I have not understood anything — not a single object; and that no man ever can.
I perceive Nature, here in sight of the sea, is taking advantage of me, to dart upon me, and sting me,
Because I have dared to open my mouth to sing at all.

To such mysticism science cannot succeed in opposing itself; it can but provide the mystic with a new leaf of the sacred writing in which spiritual truths are recorded.

Only (for me, at any rate, in all my prose and poetry), joyfully accepting modern science, and loyally following it without the slightest hesitation, there remains ever recognised still a higher flight, a higher fact, the Eternal Soul of Man, (of all else too), the Spiritual, the Religious — which it is to be the greatest office of scientism, in my opinion, and of future poetry also, to free from fables, crudities and superstitions, and launch forth in renewed faith and scope a hundred fold. To me the worlds of Religiousness, and of the conception of the Divine and of the Ideal, though mainly latent, are just as absolute in Humanity and the Universe as the world of Chemistry, or anything in the objective world. . . . To me the crown of Savantism is that it opens the way for a more splendid Theology and for ampler and diviner songs.

If Whitman seems suspicious of any class of men disposed to be antagonistic to any, it is to those whose lives are spent among books, who are not in contact with external nature, and the stir and movement of human activity, but who receive things already prepared, or, as Whitman expresses it, "distilled." He knows that the distillations are delightful, and would intoxicate himself also, but he will not let them. Rather he chooses to "lean and loafe at his ease, observing a spear of summer grass," to drink the open air (that is, everything natural and unelaborated); he is "enamoured of growing out-doors." At the same time his most ardent aspiration is after a new literature, accordant with scientific conceptions, and the feelings which correspond with democracy. And to the literature of the old world and of feudalism he willingly does justice. "American students may well derive from all former lands, . . . from witty and warlike France, and markedly, and in many ways, and at many different periods, from the enterprise and soul of the great Spanish race, bearing ourselves always courteous, always deferential, indebted beyond measure to the mother-world, to all its nations dead, as to all its nations living — the offspring, this America of ours, the daughter not by any means of the British Isles exclusively, but of the Continent, and of all continents." True culture and learning Whitman venerates; but he suspects men of refinement and polite letters and dainty information, the will-o'-the-wisps of Goethe's "Mährchen," who "lose themselves in countless masses of adjustments," who end by becoming little better than "supercilious infidels," whose culture, as Carlyle long since observed, is of a "sceptical-destructive" kind.

Men of every class then are interesting to Whitman. But no individual is pre-eminently interesting to him. His sketches of individual men and women, though wonderfully vivid and precise, are none of them longer than a page; each single figure passes rapidly out of sight, and a stream of other figures of men and women succeeds. Even in "Lincoln's Burial Hymn" he has only a word to say of "the large sweet soul that has gone;" the chords of his nocturne, with their implicated threefold sweetness, odour and sound and light, having passed into his strain, really speak not of Lincoln but of death. George Peabody is celebrated briefly, because through him, "a stintless, lavish giver, tallying the gifts of earth," a multitude of human beings have been blessed, and the true service of riches illustrated. No single person is the subject of Whitman's song, or can be;

the individual suggests a group, and the group a multitude, each unit of which is as interesting as every other unit, and possesses equal claims to recognition. Hence the recurring tendency of his poems to become catalogues of persons and things. Selection seems forbidden to him; if he names one race of mankind the names of all other races press into his page; if he mentions one trade or occupation, all other trades and occupations follow. A long procession of living forms passes before him; each several form, keenly inspected for a moment, is then dismissed. Men and women are seen *en masse,* and the mass is viewed not from a distance, but close at hand, where it is felt to be a concourse of individuals. Whitman will not have the people appear in his poems by representatives or delegates; the people itself, in its undiminished totality, marches through his poems, making its greatness and variety felt. Writing down the headings of a Trades' Directory is not poetry; but this is what Whitman never does. . . .

One can perceive at a glance that these characteristics of Whitman's work proceed directly from the democratic tendencies of the world of thought and feeling in which he moves. It is curious to find De Tocqueville, before there existed properly any native American literature, describing in the spirit of philosophical prophecy what we find realized in Whitman's "Leaves of Grass": [a quotation from Tocqueville follows.]

The democratic poet celebrates no individual hero, nor does he celebrate himself. "I celebrate myself," sings Whitman, and the longest poem in "Leaves of Grass" is named by his own name; but the self-celebration throughout is celebration of himself as a man and an American; it is what he possesses in common with all others that he feels to be glorious and worthy of song, not that which differentiates him from others; manhood, and in particular American manhood, is the real subject of the poem "Walt Whitman"; and although Whitman has a most poignant feeling of personality, which indeed is a note of all he has written, it is to be remembered that in nearly every instance in which he speaks of himself the reference is as much impersonal as personal. In what is common he finds what is most precious. The true hero of the democratic poet is the nation of which he is a member, or the whole race of man to which the nation belongs. The mettlesome, proud, turbulent, brave, self-asserting young Achilles, lover of women and lover of comrades of Whitman's epic, can be no other than the American people; the Ulysses, the prudent, the 'cute, the battler with the forces of nature, the traveller in sea-like prairie, desolate swamp, and dense forest is brother Jonathan. But if the American nation is his hero, let it be observed that it is the American nation as the supposed leader of the human race, as the supposed possessor in ideas, in type of character, and in tendency if not in actual achievement of all that is most powerful and promising for the progress of mankind. . . .

John Jay Chapman: THE SOUL OF THE TRAMP

"One result of scholars and scholarship," wrote John Jay Chapman (1862–1933), "is to interpose a phalanx of inferior minds between the young intelligence and the great wits of the past." Chapman was an exceptionally independent essayist, critic, and translator. He was not a professor or, in the narrow sense of the word, a scholar. But he was a gifted "critic of culture," a conscientious intellectual after Emerson's prescription for the American scholar as, quite simply, man thinking. His skeptical view of Whitman would find strong support among the formalist or "new critical" scholars of today.

IT would be an ill turn for an essay-writer to destroy Walt Whitman, — for he was discovered by the essayists, and but for them his notoriety would have been postponed for fifty years. He is the mare's nest of "American Literature," and scarce a contributor to *The Saturday Review* but has at one time or another raised a flag over him.

The history of these chronic discoveries of Whitman as a poet, as a force, as a something or a somebody, would write up into the best possible monograph on the incompetency of the Anglo-Saxon in matters of criticism.

English literature is the literature of genius, and the Englishman is the great creator. His work outshines the genius of Greece. His wealth outvalues the combined wealth of all modern Europe. The English mind is the only unconscious mind the world has ever seen. And for this reason the English mind is incapable of criticism.

From *The Selected Writings of John Jay Chapman,* ed. by Jacques Barzun, copyright 1957 by Farrar, Straus and Cudahy, Inc. Used by permission of the publishers, Farrar, Straus and Cudahy, Inc.

There has never been an English critic of the first rank, hardly a critic of any rank; and the critical work of England consists either of an academical bandying of a few old canons and shibboleths out of Horace or Aristotle, or else of the merest impressionism, and wordy struggle to convey the sentiment awakened by the thing studied.

Now, true criticism means an attempt to find out what something is, not for the purpose of judging it, or of imitating it, nor for the purpose of illustrating something else, nor for any other ulterior purpose whatever.

The so-called canons of criticism are of about as much service to a student of literature as the Nicene Creed and the Lord's Prayer are to the student of church history. They are a part of his subject, of course, but if he insists upon using them as a tape measure and a divining-rod he will produce a judgment of no possible value to any one, and interesting only as a record of a most complex state of mind.

The educated gentlemen of England have surveyed literature with these time-honored old instruments, and hordes of them long ago rushed to America with their theodolites and their quadrants in their hands. They sized us up and they sized us down, and they never could find greatness in literature among us till Walt Whitman appeared and satisfied the astrologers.

Here was a comet, a man of the people, a new man, who spoke no known language, who was very uncouth and insulting, who proclaimed himself a "barbaric yawp," and who corresponded to the English imagination with the unpleasant and rampant wildness of everything in America, — with Mormonism and car factories, steamboat explosions, strikes,

repudiation, and whiskey; whose form violated every one of their minor canons as America violated every one of their social ideas.

Then, too, Whitman arose out of the war, as Shakespeare arose out of the destruction of the Armada, as the Greek poets arose out of the repulse of the Persians. It was impossible, it was unprecedented, that a national revulsion should not produce national poetry — and lo! here was Whitman.

It may safely be said that the discovery of Whitman as a poet caused many a hard-thinking Oxford man to sleep quietly at night. America was solved.

The Englishman travels, but he travels after his mind has been burnished by the university, and at an age when the best he can do in the line of thought is to make an intelligent manipulation of the few notions he leaves home with. He departs an educated gentleman, taking with him his portmanteau and his ideas. He returns a travelled gentleman, bringing with him his ideas and his portmanteau. He would as soon think of getting his coats from Kansas as his thoughts from travel. And therefore every impression of America which the travelling Englishman experienced confirmed his theory of Whitman. Even Rudyard Kipling, who does not in any sense fall under the above description, has enough Anglo-Saxon blood in him to see in this country only the fulfilment of the fantastic notions of his childhood.

But imagine an Oxford man who had eyes in his head, and who should come to this country, never having heard of Whitman. He would see an industrious and narrow-minded population, commonplace and monotonous, so uniform that one man can hardly be distinguished from another, law-abiding, timid, and traditional; a community where the individual is suppressed by law, custom, and instinct, and in which, by consequence, there are few or no great men, even counting those men thrust by necessary operation of the laws of trade into commercial prominence, and who claim scientific rather than personal notice.

The culture of this people, its architecture, letters, drama, etc., he would find were, of necessity, drawn from European models; and in its poetry, so far as poetry existed, he would recognize a somewhat feeble imitation of English poetry. The newspaper verses very fairly represent the average talent for poetry and average appreciation of it, and the newspaper verse of the United States is precisely what one would expect from a decorous and unimaginative population — intelligent, conservative, and uninspired.

Above the newspaper versifiers float the minor poets, and above these soar the greater poets; and the characteristics of the whole hierarchy are the same as those of the humblest acolyte — intelligence, conservatism, conventional morality.

Above the atmosphere they live in, above the heads of all the American poets, and between them and the sky, float the Constitution of the United States and the traditions and forms of English literature.

This whole culture is secondary and tertiary, and it truly represents the respectable mediocrity from which it emanates. Whittier and Longfellow have been much read in their day — read by mill-hands and clerks and school-teachers, by lawyers and doctors and divines, by the reading classes of the republic, whose ideals they truly spoke for, whose yearnings and spiritual life they truly expressed.

Now, the Oxford traveller would not have found Whitman at all. He would never have met a man who had heard of him, nor seen a man like him.

The traveller, as he opened his *Saturday Review* upon his return to London, and read the current essay on Whitman, would have been faced by a problem fit to puzzle Montesquieu, a problem to floor Goethe.

And yet Whitman is representative. He is a real product, he has a real and most interesting place in the history of literature, and he speaks for a class and type of human nature whose interest is more than local, whose prevalence is admitted — a type which is one of the products of the civilization of the century, perhaps of all centuries, and which has a positively planetary significance.

There are, in every country, individuals who, after a sincere attempt to take a place in organized society, revolt from the drudgery of it, content themselves with the simplest satisfactions of the grossest need of nature, so far as subsistence is concerned, and rediscover the infinite pleasures of life in the open air.

If the roadside, the sky, the distant town, the soft buffeting of the winds of heaven, are a joy to the aesthetic part of man, the freedom from all responsibility and accountability is Nirvana to his moral nature. A man who has once tasted these two joys together, the joy of being in the open air and the joy of being disreputable and unashamed, has touched an experience which the most close-knit and determined nature might well dread. Life has no terrors for such a man. Society has no hold on him. The trifling inconveniences of the mode of life are as nothing compared with its satisfactions. The worm that never dies is dead in him. The great mystery of consciousness and of effort is quietly dissolved into the vacant happiness of sensation — not base sensation, but the sensation of the dawn and the sunset, of the mart and the theatre, and the stars, the panorama of the universe.

To the moral man, to the philosopher or the business man, to any one who is a cog in the wheel of some republic, all these things exist for the sake of something else. He must explain or make use of them, or define his relation to them. He spends the whole agony of his existence in an endeavor to docket them and deal with them. Hampered as he is by all that has been said and done before, he yet feels himself driven on to summarize, and wreak himself upon the impossible task of grasping this cosmos with his mind, of holding it in his hand, of subordinating it to his purpose.

The tramp is freed from all this. By an act as simple as death, he has put off effort and lives in peace.

It is no wonder that every country in Europe shows myriads of these men, as it shows myriads of suicides annually. It is no wonder, though the sociologists have been late in noting it, that specimens of the type are strikingly identical in feature in every country of the globe.

The habits, the physique, the tone of mind, even the sign-language and some of the catchwords, of tramps are the same everywhere. The men are not natally outcasts. They have always tried civilized life. Their early training, at least their early attitude of mind towards life, has generally been respectable. That they should be criminally inclined goes without saying, because their minds have been freed from the sanctions which enforce law. But their general innocence is, under the circumstances, very remarkable, and distinguishes them from the criminal classes.

When we see one of these men sitting on a gate, or sauntering down a city street, how often have we wondered how life appeared to him; what solace and what problems it presented. How often have we longed to know the history of such a soul, told, not by the police-blotter, but by the poet or novelist in the heart of the man!

Walt Whitman has given utterance to the soul of the tramp. A man of genius has passed sincerely and normally through this entire experience, himself unconscious of what he was, and has left a record of it to enlighten and bewilder the literary world.

In Whitman's works the elemental parts of a man's mind and the fragments of imperfect education may be seen merging together, floating and sinking in a sea of insensate egotism and rhapsody, repellent, divine, disgusting, extraordinary.

Our inability to place the man intellectually, and find a type and reason for his intellectual state, comes from this: that the revolt he represents is not an intellectual revolt. Ideas are not at the bottom of it. It is a revolt from drudgery. It is the revolt of laziness.

There is no intellectual coherence in his talk, but merely pathological coherence. Can the insulting jumble of ignorance and effrontery, of scientific phrase and French paraphrase, of slang and inspired adjective, which he puts forward with the pretence that it represents thought, be regarded, from any possible point of view, as a philosophy, or a system, or a belief? Is it individualism of any statable kind? Do the thoughts and phrases which float about in it have a meaning which bears any relation to the meaning they bear in the language of thinkers? Certainly not. Does all the patriotic talk, the talk about the United States and its future, have any significance as patriotism? Does it poetically represent the state of feeling of any class of American citizens towards their country? Or would you find the nearest equivalent to this emotion in the breast of the educated tramp of France, or Germany, or England? The speech of Whitman is English, and his metaphors and catchwords are apparently American, but the emotional content is cosmic. He put off patriotism when he took to the road.

The attraction exercised by his writings is due to their flashes of reality. Of course the man was a poseur, a most horrid mountebank and ego-maniac. His tawdry scraps of misused idea, of literary smartness, of dog-eared and greasy reminiscence, repel us. The world of men remained for him as his audience, and he did to civilized society the continuous compliment of an insane self-consciousness in its presence.

Perhaps this egotism and posturing is the revenge of a stilled conscience, and we ought to read in it the inversion of the social instincts. Perhaps all tramps are poseurs. But there is this to be said for Whitman, that whether or not his posing was an accident of a personal nature, or an organic result of his life, he was himself an authentic creature. He did not sit in a study and throw off his saga of balderdash, but he lived a life, and it is by his authenticity, and not by his poses, that he has survived.

The descriptions of nature, the visual observation of life, are first-hand and wonderful. It was no false light that led the Oxonians to call some of his phrases Homeric. The pundits were right in their curiosity over him; they went astray only in their attempt at classification.

It is a pity that truth and beauty turn to cant on the second delivery, for it makes poetry, as a profession, impossible.

The lyric poets have always spent most of their time in trying to write lyric poetry, and the very attempt disqualifies them.

A poet who discovers his mission is already half done for; and even Wordsworth, great genius though he was, succeeded in half drowning his talents in his parochial theories, in his own self-consciousness and self-conceit.

Walt Whitman thought he had a mission. He was a professional poet. He had purposes and theories about poetry which he started out to enforce and illustrate. He is as didactic as Wordsworth, and is thinking of himself the whole time. He belonged, moreover, to that class of professionals who are always particularly self-centred, autocratic, vain, and florid — the class of quacks. There are, throughout society, men, and they are generally men of unusual natural powers, who, after gaining a little unassimilated education, launch out for themselves and set up as authorities on their own account. They are, perhaps, the successors of the old astrologers, in that what they seek to establish is some personal professorship or predominance. The old occultism and mystery was resorted to as the most obvious device for increasing the personal importance of the magician; and the chief difference today between a regular physician and a quack is, that the quack pretends to know it all.

Brigham Young and Joseph Smith were men of phenomenal capacity, who actually invented a religion and created a community by the apparent establishment of supernatural and occult powers. The phrenologists, the venders of patent medicine, the Christian Scientists, the single-taxers, and all who proclaim panaceas and nostrums make the same majestic and pontifical appeal to human nature. It is this mystical power, this religious element, which floats them, sells the drugs, cures the sick, and packs the meetings.

By temperament and education Walt Whitman was fitted to be a prophet of this kind. He became a quack poet, and hampered his talents by the imposition of a monstrous parade of rattletrap theories and professions. If he had not been endowed with a perfectly marvellous capacity, a wealth of nature beyond the reach and plumb of his rodomontade, he would have been ruined from the start. As it is, he has filled his work with grimace and vulgarity. He writes a few lines of epic directness and cyclopean vigor and naturalness, and then obtrudes himself and his mission.

He has the bad taste bred in the bone of all missionaries and palmists, the sign-manual of a true quack. This bad taste is nothing more than the offensive intrusion of himself and his mission into the matter in hand. As for his real merits and his true mission, too much can hardly be said in his favor. The field of his experience was narrow, and not in the least intellectual. It was narrow because of his isolation from human life. A poet like Browning, or Heine, or Alfred de Musset deals constantly with the problems and struggles that arise in civilized life out of the close relationships, the ties, the duties and desires of the human heart. He explains life on its social side. He gives us some more or less coherent view of an infinitely complicated matter. He is a guidebook or a notebook, a highly trained and intelligent companion.

Walt Whitman has no interest in any of these things. He was fortunately so very ignorant and untrained that his mind was utterly incoherent and unintellectual. His mind seems to be submerged and to have become almost a part of his body. The utter lack of con-

centration which resulted from living his whole life in the open air has left him spontaneous and unaccountable. And the great value of his work is, that it represents the spontaneous and unaccountable functioning of the mind and body in health.

It is doubtful whether a man ever enjoyed life more intensely than Walt Whitman, or expressed the physical joy of mere living more completely. He is robust, all tingling with health and the sensations of health. All that is best in his poetry is the expression of bodily well-being.

A man who leaves his office and gets into a canoe on a Canadian river, sure of ten days' release from the cares of business and housekeeping, has a thrill of joy such as Walt Whitman has here and there thrown into his poetry. One might say that to have done this is the greatest accomplishment in literature. Walt Whitman, in some of his lines, breaks the frame of poetry and gives us life in the throb.

It is the throb of the whole physical system of a man who breathes the open air and feels the sky over him. "When lilacs last in the dooryard bloomed" is a great lyric. Here is a whole poem without a trace of self-consciousness. It is little more than a description of nature. The allusions to Lincoln and to the funeral are but a word or two — merest suggestions of the tragedy. But grief, overwhelming grief, is in every line of it, the grief which has been transmuted into this sensitiveness to the landscape, to the song of the thrush, to the lilac's bloom, and the sunset.

Here is truth to life of the kind to be found in King Lear or Guy Mannering, in Aeschylus or Burns.

Walt Whitman himself could not have told you why the poem was good. Had he had any intimation of the true reason, he would have spoiled the poem. The recurrence and antiphony of the thrush, the lilac, the thought of death, the beauty of nature, are in a balance and dream of natural symmetry such as no cunning could come at, no conscious art could do other than spoil.

It is ungrateful to note Whitman's limitations, his lack of human passion, the falseness of many of his notions about the American people. The man knew the world merely as an observer, he was never a living part of it, and no mere observer can understand the life about him. Even his work during the war was mainly the work of an observer, and his poems and notes upon the period are picturesque. As to his talk about comrades and Manhattanese car-drivers, and brass-founders displaying their brawny arms round each other's brawny necks, all this gush and sentiment in Whitman's poetry is false to life. It has a lyrical value, as representing Whitman's personal feelings, but no one else in the country was ever found who felt or acted like this.

In fact, in all that concerns the human relations Walt Whitman is as unreal, as, let us say, William Morris, and the American mechanic would probably prefer Sigurd the Volsung, and understand it better than Whitman's poetry.

This falseness to the sentiment of the American is interwoven with such wonderful descriptions of American sights and scenery, of ferryboats, thoroughfares, cataracts, and machine-shops that it is not strange the foreigners should have accepted the gospel.

On the whole, Whitman, though he solves none of the problems of life and throws no light on American civilization, is a delightful appearance, and a strange creature to come out of our beehive. This man committed every unpardonable sin against our conventions, and his whole life was an outrage. He was neither chaste, nor industrious, nor religious. He patiently lived upon cold pie and tramped the earth in triumph.

He did really live the life he liked to live, in defiance of all men, and this is a great desert, a most stirring merit. And he gave, in his writings, a true picture of himself and of that life — a picture which the world had never seen before, and which it is probable the world will not soon cease to wonder at.

George Santayana: THE POETRY OF BARBARISM

*George Santayana (1863–1952), the Harvard philosopher, was
born in Spain and brought up in Boston. He looks at American life
from a catholic, European angle of vision. Elsewhere he defines the
essence of the American character as that of "an idealist working on
matter." The typical American, says Santayana, is a good workman
who "hardly distinguishes his artistic intention from the potency in
himself and in things. . . . Accordingly his ideals fall into the form of
premonitions and prophecies. . . ." Santayana's essay remains the most
trenchant of many critical attacks upon Whitman.*

I

IT is an observation at first sight melancholy but in the end, perhaps, enlightening, that the earliest poets are the most ideal, and that primitive ages furnish the most heroic characters and have the clearest vision of a perfect life. The Homeric times must have been full of ignorance and suffering. In those little barbaric towns, in those camps and farms, in those shipyards, there must have been much insecurity and superstition. That age was singularly poor in all that concerns the convenience of life and the entertainment of the mind with arts and sciences. Yet it had a sense for civilization. That machinery of life which men were beginning to devise appealed to them as poetical; they knew its ultimate justification and studied its incipient processes with delight. The poetry of that simple and ignorant age was, accordingly, the sweetest and sanest that the world has known; the most faultless in taste, and the most even and lofty in inspiration. Without lacking variety and homeliness, it bathed all things human in the golden light of morning; it clothed sorrow in a kind of majesty, instinct with both self-control and heroic frankness. Nowhere else can we find so noble a rendering of human nature, so spontaneous a delight in life, so uncompromising a dedication to beauty, and such a gift of seeing beauty in everything. Homer, the first of poets, was also the best and the most poetical.

From this beginning, if we look down the history of Occidental literature, we see the power of idealization steadily decline. For while it finds here and there, as in Dante, a more spiritual theme and a subtler and riper intellect, it pays for that advantage by a more than equivalent loss in breadth, sanity, and happy vigour. And if ever imagination bursts out with a greater potency, as in Shakespeare (who excels the patriarch of poetry in depth of passion and vividness of characterization, and in those exquisite bubblings of poetry and humour in which English genius is at its best), yet Shakespeare also pays the price by a notable loss in taste, in sustained inspiration, in consecration, and in rationality. There is more or less rubbish in his greatest works. When we come down to our own day we find poets of hardly less natural endowment (for in endowment all ages

From *Interpretations of Poetry and Religion,* by George Santayana (New York, 1900, Charles Scribner's Sons), pp. 166–187.

are perhaps alike) and with vastly richer
sources of inspiration; for they have
many arts and literatures behind them,
with the spectacle of a varied and agi-
tated society, a world which is the living
microcosm of its own history and presents in one picture many races, arts, and
religions. Our poets have more wonderful tragedies of the imagination to depict
than had Homer, whose world was innocent of any essential defeat, or Dante,
who believed in the world's definitive
redemption. Or, if perhaps their inspiration is comic, they have the pageant of
mediaeval manners, with its picturesque
artifices and passionate fancies, and the
long comedy of modern social revolu-
tions, so illusory in their aims and so pro-
ductive in their aimlessness. They have,
moreover, the new and marvellous conception which natural science has given
us of the world and of the conditions of
human progress.

With all these lessons of experience
behind them, however, we find our contemporary poets incapable of any high
wisdom, incapable of any imaginative
rendering of human life and its meaning.
Our poets are things of shreds and
patches; they give up episodes and studies, a sketch of this curiosity, a glimpse
of that romance; they have no total
vision, no grasp of the whole reality, and
consequently no capacity for a sane and
steady idealization. The comparatively
barbarous ages had a poetry of the ideal;
they had visions of beauty, order, and
perfection. This age of material elaboration has no sense for those things. Its
fancy is retrospective, whimsical, and
flickering; its ideals, when it has any, are
negative and partial; its moral strength
is a blind and miscellaneous vehemence.
Its poetry, in a word, is the poetry of
barbarism.

This poetry should be viewed in relation to the general moral crisis and imaginative disintegration of which it gives a
verbal echo; then we shall avoid the in-
justice of passing it over as insignificant,
no less than the imbecility of hailing it
as essentially glorious and successful. We
must remember that the imagination of
our race has been subject to a double
discipline. It has been formed partly in
the school of classic literature and polity,
and partly in the school of Christian
piety. This duality of inspiration, this
contradiction between the two accepted
methods of rationalizing the world, has
been a chief source of that incoherence,
that romantic indistinctness and imper-
fection, which largely characterize the
products of the modern arts. A man cannot serve two masters; yet the conditions
have not been such as to allow him
wholly to despise the one or wholly to
obey the other. To be wholly Pagan is
impossible after the dissolution of that
civilization which had seemed universal,
and that empire which had believed itself eternal. To be wholly Christian is
impossible for a similar reason, now that
the illusion and cohesion of Christian
ages is lost, and for the further reason
that Christianity was itself fundamentally eclectic. Before it could succeed
and dominate men even for a time, it
was obliged to adjust itself to reality, to
incorporate many elements of Pagan wisdom, and to accommodate itself to many
habits and passions at variance with its
own ideal.

In these latter times, with the prodigious growth of material life in elaboration and of mental life in diffusion, there
has supervened upon this old dualism a
new faith in man's absolute power, a kind
of return to the inexperience and self-
assurance of youth. This new inspiration
has made many minds indifferent to the
two traditional disciplines; neither is seri-

ously accepted by them, for the reason, excellent from their own point of view, that no discipline whatever is needed. The memory of ancient disillusions has faded with time. Ignorance of the past has bred contempt for the lessons which the past might teach. Men prefer to repeat the old experiment without knowing that they repeat it.

I say advisedly ignorance of the past, in spite of the unprecedented historical erudition of our time; for life is an art not to be learned by observation, and the most minute and comprehensive studies do not teach us what the spirit of man should have learned by its long living. We study the past as a dead object, as a ruin, not as an authority and as an experiment. One reason why history was less interesting to former ages was that they were less conscious of separation from the past. The perspective of time was less clear because the synthesis of experience was more complete. The mind does not easily discriminate the successive phases of an action in which it is still engaged; it does not arrange in a temporal series the elements of a single perception, but posits them all together as constituting a permanent and real object. Human nature and the life of the world were real and stable objects to the apprehension of our forefathers; the actors changed, but not the characters or the play. Men were then less studious of derivations because they were more conscious of identities. They thought of all reality as in a sense contemporary, and in considering the maxims of a philosopher or the style of a poet, they were not primarily concerned with settling his date and describing his environment. The standard by which they judged was eternal; the environment in which man found himself did not seem to them subject of any essential change.

To us the picturesque element in history is more striking because we feel ourselves the children of our own age only, an age which being itself singular and revolutionary, tends to read its own character into the past, and to regard all other periods as no less fragmentary and effervescent than itself. The changing and the permanent elements are, indeed, everywhere present, and the bias of the observer may emphasize the one or the other as it will: the only question is whether we find the significance of things in their variations or in their similarities.

Now the habit of regarding the past as effete and as merely a stepping-stone to something present or future, is unfavourable to any true apprehension of that element in the past which was vital and which remains eternal. It is a habit of thought that destroys the sense of the moral identity of all ages, by virtue of its very insistence on the mechanical derivation of one age from another. Existences that cause one another exclude one another; each is alien to the rest inasmuch as it is the product of new and different conditions. Ideas that cause nothing unite all things by giving them a common point of reference and a single standard of value.

The classic and the Christian systems were both systems of ideas, attempts to seize the eternal morphology of reality and describe its unchanging constitution. The imagination was summoned thereby to contemplate the highest objects, and the essence of things being thus described, their insignificant variations could retain little importance and the study of these variations might well seem superficial. Mechanical science, the science of causes, was accordingly neglected, while the science of values, with the arts that express these values, was exclusively pursued. The reverse has now occurred and the spirit of life, innocent of any rationalizing discipline and deprived of an authoritative and adequate method of expression, has relapsed into miscellaneous and shallow exuberance. Religion and art have become short-winded. They have forgotten the old maxim that we should copy in order to be copied and remember in order to be remembered. It is true that the multiplicity of these incompetent efforts seems to many a compensation for their ill success, or even a ground for asserting their absolute superiority. Incompetence, when it flatters the passions, can always find a greater incompetence to approve of it. Indeed, some people would have regarded the Tower of Babel as the best academy of eloquence on account of the variety of oratorical methods prevailing there.

It is thus that the imagination of our time has relapsed into barbarism. But discipline of the heart and fancy is always so rare a thing that the neglect of it need not be supposed to involve any very terrible or obvious loss. The triumphs of reason have been few and partial at any time, and perfect works of art are almost unknown. The failure of art and reason, because their principle is ignored, is therefore hardly more conspicuous than it was when their principle, although perhaps acknowledged, was misunderstood or disobeyed. Indeed, to one who fixes his eye on the ideal goal, the greatest art often seems the greatest failure, because it alone reminds him of what it should have been. Trivial stimulations coming from vulgar objects, on the contrary, by making us forget altogether the possibility of a deep satisfaction, often succeed in interesting and in winning applause. The pleasure they give us is so brief and superficial that

the wave of essential disappointment which would ultimately drown it has not time to rise from the heart.

The poetry of barbarism is not without its charm. It can play with sense and passion the more readily and freely in that it does not aspire to subordinate them to a clear thought or a tenable attitude of the will. It can impart the transitive emotions which it expresses; it can find many partial harmonies of mood and fancy; it can, by virtue of its red-hot irrationality, utter wilder cries, surrender itself and us to more absolute passion, and heap up a more indiscriminate wealth of images than belong to poets of seasoned experience or of heavenly inspiration. Irrational stimulation may tire us in the end, but it excites us in the beginning; and how many conventional poets, tender and prolix, have there not been, who tire us now without ever having excited anybody? The power to stimulate is the beginning of greatness, and when the barbarous poet has genius, as he well may have, he stimulates all the more powerfully on account of the crudity of his methods and the recklessness of his emotions. The defects of such art — lack of distinction, absence of beauty, confusion of ideas, incapacity permanently to please — will hardly be felt by the contemporary public, if once its attention is arrested; for no poet is so undisciplined that he will not find many readers, if he finds readers at all, less disciplined than himself.

These considerations may perhaps be best enforced by applying them to two writers of great influence over the present generation who seem to illustrate them on different planes — Robert Browning and Walt Whitman. They are both analytic poets — poets who seek to reveal and express the elemental as opposed to the conventional; but the dissolution has progressed much farther in Whitman than in Browning, doubtless because Whitman began at a much lower stage of moral and intellectual organization; for the good will to be radical was present in both. The elements to which Browning reduces experience are still passions, characters, persons; Whitman carries the disintegration further and knows nothing but moods and particular images. The world of Browning is a world of history with civilization for its setting and with the conventional passions for its motive forces. The world of Whitman is innocent of these things and contains only far simpler and more chaotic elements. In him the barbarism is much more pronounced; it is, indeed, avowed, and the "barbaric yawp" is sent "over the roofs of the world" in full consciousness of its inarticulate character; but in Browning the barbarism is no less real though disguised by a literary and scientific language, since the passions of civilized life with which he deals are treated as so many "barbaric yawps," complex indeed in their conditions, puffings of an intricate engine, but aimless in their vehemence and mere ebullitions of lustiness in adventurous and profoundly ungoverned souls.

Irrationality on this level is viewed by Browning with the same satisfaction with which, on a lower level, it is viewed by Whitman; and the admirers of each hail it as the secret of a new poetry which pierces to the quick and awakens the imagination to a new and genuine vitality. It is in the rebellion against discipline, in the abandonment of the ideals of classic and Christian tradition, that this rejuvenation is found. Both poets represent, therefore, and are admired for representing, what may be called the poetry of barbarism in the most accurate and descriptive sense of this word. For

the barbarian is the man who regards his passions as their own excuse for being; who does not domesticate them either by understanding their cause or by conceiving their ideal goal. He is the man who does not know his derivations nor perceive his tendencies, but who merely feels and acts, valuing in his life its force and its filling, but being careless of its purpose and its form. His delight is in abundance and vehemence; his art, like his life, shows an exclusive respect for quantity and splendour of materials. His scorn for what is poorer and weaker than himself is only surpassed by his ignorance of what is higher.

II

WALT WHITMAN

The works of Walt Whitman offer an extreme illustration of this phase of genius, both by their form and by their substance. It was the singularity of his literary form — the challenge it threw to the conventions of verse and of language — that first gave Whitman notoriety: but this notoriety has become fame, because those incapacities and solecisms which glare at us from his pages are only the obverse of a profound inspiration and of a genuine courage. Even the idiosyncrasies of his style have a side which is not mere perversity or affectation; the order of his words, the procession of his images, reproduce the method of a rich, spontaneous, absolutely lazy fancy. In most poets such a natural order is modified by various governing motives — the thought, the metrical form, the echo of other poems in the memory. By Walt Whitman these conventional influences are resolutely banished. We find the swarms of men and objects rendered as they might strike the retina in a sort of waking dream. It is the most sincere possible confession of the lowest — I mean the most primitive — type of perception. All ancient poets are sophisticated in comparison and give proof of longer intellectual and moral training. Walt Whitman has gone back to the innocent style of Adam, when the animals filed before him one by one and he called each of them by its name.

In fact, the influences to which Walt Whitman was subject were as favourable as possible to the imaginary experiment of beginning the world over again. Liberalism and transcendentalism both harboured some illusions on that score; and they were in the air which our poet breathed. Moreover he breathed this air in America, where the newness of the material environment made it easier to ignore the fatal antiquity of human nature. When he afterward became aware that there was or had been a world with a history, he studied that world with curiosity and spoke of it not without a certain shrewdness. But he still regarded it as a foreign world and imagined, as not a few Americans have done, that his own world was a fresh creation, not amenable to the same laws as the old. The difference in the conditions blinded him, in his merely sensuous apprehension, to the identity of the principles.

His parents were farmers in central Long Island and his early years were spent in that district. The family seems to have been not too prosperous and somewhat nomadic; Whitman himself drifted through boyhood without much guidance. We find him now at school, now helping the labourers at the farms, now wandering along the beaches of Long Island, finally at Brooklyn working in an apparently desultory way as a printer and sometimes as a writer for a local newspaper. He must have read or

heard something, at this early period, of the English classics; his style often betrays the deep effect made upon him by the grandiloquence of the Bible, of Shakespeare, and of Milton. But his chief interest, if we may trust his account, was already in his own sensations. The aspects of Nature, the forms and habits of animals, the sights of cities, the movement and talk of common people, were his constant delight. His mind was flooded with these images, keenly felt and afterward to be vividly rendered with bold strokes of realism and imagination.

Many poets have had this faculty to seize the elementary aspects of things, but none has had it so exclusively; with Whitman the surface is absolutely all and the underlying structure is without interest and almost without existence. He had had no education and his natural delight in imbibing sensations had not been trained to the uses of practical or theoretical intelligence. He basked in the sunshine of perception and wallowed in the stream of his own sensibility, as later at Camden in the shallows of his favourite brook. Even during the civil war, when he heard the drum-taps so clearly, he could only gaze at the picturesque and terrible aspects of the struggle, and linger among the wounded day after day with a canine devotion; he could not be aroused either to clear thought or to positive action. So also in his poems; a multiplicity of images pass before him and he yields himself to each in turn with absolute passivity. The world has no inside; it is a phantasmagoria of continuous visions, vivid, impressive, but monotonous and hard to distinguish in memory, like the waves of the sea or the decorations of some barbarous temple, sublime only by the infinite aggregation of parts.

This abundance of detail without organization, this wealth of perception without intelligence and of imagination without taste, makes the singularity of Whitman's genius. Full of sympathy and receptivity, with a wonderful gift of graphic characterization and an occasional rare grandeur of diction, he fills us with a sense of the individuality and the universality of what he describes — it is a drop in itself yet a drop in the ocean. The absence of any principle of selection or of a sustained style enables him to render aspects of things and of emotion which would have eluded a trained writer. He is, therefore, interesting even where he is grotesque or perverse. He has accomplished, by the sacrifice of almost every other good quality, something never so well done before. He has approached common life without bringing in his mind any higher standard by which to criticise it; he has seen it, not in contrast with an ideal, but as the expression of forces more indeterminate and elementary than itself; and the vulgar, in this cosmic setting, has appeared to him sublime.

There is clearly some analogy between a mass of images without structure and the notion of an absolute democracy. Whitman, inclined by his genius and habits to see life without relief or organization, believed that his inclination in this respect corresponded with the spirit of his age and country, and that Nature and society, at least in the United States, were constituted after the fashion of his own mind. Being the poet of the average man, he wished all men to be specimens of that average, and being the poet of a fluid Nature, he believed that Nature was or should be a formless flux. This personal bias of Whitman's was further encouraged by the actual absence of distinction in his immediate environment.

Surrounded by ugly things and common people, he felt himself happy, ecstatic, overflowing with a kind of patriarchal love. He accordingly came to think that there was a spirit of the New World which he embodied, and which was in complete opposition to that of the Old, and that a literature upon novel principles was needed to express and strengthen this American spirit.

Democracy was not to be merely a constitutional device for the better government of given nations, nor merely a movement for the material improvement of the lot of the poorer classes. It was to be a social and a moral democracy and to involve an actual equality among all men. Whatever kept them apart and made it impossible for them to be messmates together was to be discarded. The literature of democracy was to ignore all extraordinary gifts of genius or virtue, all distinction drawn even from great passions or romantic adventures. In Whitman's works, in which this new literature is foreshadowed, there is accordingly not a single character nor a single story. His only hero is Myself, the "single separate person," endowed with the primary impulses, with health, and with sensitiveness to the elementary aspects of Nature. The perfect man of the future, the prolific begetter of other perfect men, is to work with his hands, chanting the poems of some future Walt, some ideally democratic bard. Women are to have as nearly as possible the same character as men: the emphasis is to pass from family life and local ties to the friendship of comrades and the general brotherhand of man. Men are to be vigorous, comfortable, sentimental, and irresponsible.

This dream is, of course, unrealized and unrealizable, in America as elsewhere. Undeniably there are in America many suggestions of such a society and such a national character. But the growing complexity and fixity of institutions necessarily tends to obscure these traits of a primitive and crude democracy. What Whitman seized upon as the promise of the future was in reality the survival of the past. He sings the song of pioneers, but it is in the nature of the pioneer that the greater his success the quicker must be his transformation into something different. When Whitman made the initial and amorphous phase of society his ideal, he became the prophet of a lost cause. That cause was lost, not merely when wealth and intelligence began to take shape in the American Commonwealth, but it was lost at the very foundation of the world, when those laws of evolution were established which Whitman, like Rousseau, failed to understand. If we may trust Mr. Herbert Spencer, these laws involve a passage from the homogeneous to the heterogeneous, and a constant progress at once in differentiation and in organization — all, in a word, that Whitman systematically deprecated or ignored. He is surely not the spokesman of the tendencies of his country, although he describes some aspects of its past and present condition: nor does he appeal to those whom he describes, but rather to the *dilettanti* he despises. He is regarded as representative chiefly by foreigners, who look for some grotesque expression of the genius of so young and prodigious a people.

Whitman, it is true, loved and comprehended men; but this love and comprehension had the same limits as his love and comprehension of Nature. He observed truly and responded to his observation with genuine and pervasive emotion. A great gregariousness, an innocent tolerance of moral weakness, a genuine admiration for bodily health and strength, made him bubble over with affection for the generic human creature. Incapable of an ideal passion, he was full of the milk of human kindness. Yet, for all his acquaintance with the ways and thoughts of the common man of his choice, he did not truly understand him. For to understand people is to go much deeper than they go themselves; to penetrate to their characters and disentangle their inmost ideals. Whitman's insight into man did not go beyond a sensuous sympathy; it consisted in a vicarious satisfaction in their pleasures, and an instinctive love of their persons. It never approached a scientific or imaginative knowledge of their hearts.

Therefore Whitman failed radically in his dearest ambition: he can never be a poet of the people. For the people, like the early races whose poetry was ideal, are natural believers in perfection. They have no doubts about the absolute desirability of wealth and learning and power, none about the worth of pure goodness and pure love. Their chosen poets, if they have any, will be always those who have known how to paint these ideals in lively even if in gaudy colours. Nothing is farther from the common people than the corrupt desire to be primitive. They instinctively look toward a more exalted life, which they imagine to be full of distinction and pleasure, and the idea of that brighter existence fills them with hope or with envy or with humble admiration.

If the people are ever won over to hostility to such ideals, it is only because they are cheated by demagogues who tell them that if all the flowers of civilization were destroyed its fruits would become more abundant. A greater share of happiness, people think, would fall to their lot could they destroy everything beyond their own possible possessions.

But they are made thus envious and ignoble only by a deception: what they really desire is an ideal good for themselves which they are told they may secure by depriving others of their pre-eminence. Their hope is always to enjoy perfect satisfaction themselves; and therefore a poet who loves the picturesque aspects of labour and vagrancy will hardly be the poet of the poor. He may have described their figure and occupation, in neither of which they are much interested; he will not have read their souls. They will prefer to him any sentimental story-teller, any sensational dramatist, any moralizing poet; for they are hero-worshippers by temperament, and are too wise or too unfortunate to be much enamoured of themselves or of the conditions of their existence.

Fortunately, the political theory that makes Whitman's principle of literary prophecy and criticism does not always inspire his chants, nor is it presented, even in his prose works, quite bare and unadorned. In "Democratic Vistas" we find it clothed with something of the same poetic passion and lighted up with the same flashes of intuition which we admire in the poems. Even there the temperament is finer than the ideas and the poet wiser than the thinker. His ultimate appeal is really to something more primitive and general than any social aspirations, to something more elementary than an ideal of any kind. He speaks to those minds and to those moods in which sensuality is touched with mysticism. When the intellect is in abeyance, when we would "turn and live with the animals, they are so placid and self-contained," when we are weary of conscience and of ambition, and would yield ourselves for a while to the dream of sense, Walt Whitman is a welcome companion. The images he arouses in us, fresh, full of light and health and of a kind of frankness and beauty, are prized all the more at such a time because they are not choice, but drawn perhaps from a hideous and sordid environment. For this circumstance makes them a better means of escape from convention and from that fatigue and despair which lurk not far beneath the surface of conventional life. In casting off with self-assurance and a sense of fresh vitality the distinctions of tradition and reason a man may feel, as he sinks back comfortably to a lower level of sense and instinct, that he is returning to Nature or escaping into the infinite. Mysticism makes us proud and happy to renounce the work of intelligence, both in thought and in life, and persuades us that we become divine by remaining imperfectly human. Walt Whitman gives a new expression to this ancient and multiform tendency. He feels his own cosmic justification and he would lend the sanction of his inspiration to all loafers and holiday-makers. He would be the congenial patron of farmers and factory hands in their crude pleasures and pieties, as Pan was the patron of the shepherds of Arcadia: for he is sure that in spite of his hairiness and animality, the gods will acknowledge him as one of themselves and smile upon him from the serenity of Olympus.

Van Wyck Brooks: THE PRECIPITANT

"Listen to the States asserting: 'The hour has struck! Americans shall be American. The U. S. A. is now grown up artistically. It is time we ceased to hang on the skirts of Europe. . . .'" When D. H. Lawrence made this pronouncement (in 1922) he might well have been thinking of America's Coming-of-Age (1915) by Van Wyck Brooks. This influential book proclaimed that America was now grown up. Of course Americans had been saying as much since Emerson's time, but Brooks restated the theme at a critical moment in our cultural history. As the following excerpt indicates, Whitman's poetry was a focal point in Brooks' conception of American culture. Brooks was born in 1886, and is best known for his Makers and Finders, a five-volume history of American literature that includes The Times of Melville and Whitman (1947).

I HAVE been trying to show in what way a survey of American literature would inevitably lead us to certain general facts about American life. I opened the survey with a statement which I think no one will contradict, that in American literature something has always been wanting, that a certain density, weight and richness, a certain poignancy, a "something far more deeply interfused," simply is not there. Beginning with this clue and reaching an axiom to which it seemed to me to lead, I suggested a certain practical conclusion as the result of our enquiry: that those of our writers who have possessed a vivid personal talent have been paralyzed by the want of a social background, while those who have possessed a vivid social talent have been equally unable to develop their personalities.

There is, I think, something in some not very vague way unsatisfactory about each of the writers we have been examining. Taken as a whole, the most characteristic fact about them is a certain delicacy which arrives in literature almost in the degree to which it stands remote from life, achieves its own salvation (after the Puritan fashion) by avoiding contact with actuality. Almost all the greater American writers, placed beside their English contemporaries, have a certain all too unworldly refinement. Purity of style and delicacy of touch at once distinguish Emerson from Carlyle, and Hawthorne from any Victorian novelist; but the abyss between their writings and the world in which they lived is immeasurably greater. The American character speaks through them, of course, but it is the American character only in its most sublimated form, carefully cleansed as it were and highly rarefied. Nothing is more marked than their disinclination to take a plunge, reckless and complete, as Carlyle and Dickens did, into the rudest and grossest actualities. The poet Camoens on his deathbed observed that his life had been spent in trying to keep himself afloat in a stormy sea, and his only care had been to exercise his left hand with double energy so that his right hand might be free to hold his *Lusiads* aloft, uncontaminated by the waves. This is the whole story of American literature: in a more than usually difficult and sordid world, it has applied its principal energies to being uncontaminated itself. It has held aloof, as a consciously better part, like all American idealism. The talent is there, high and dry; and if it is not always too high, it is very often a great deal too dry.

In fact, we have in America two publics, the cultivated public and the business public, the public of theory and the public of activity, the public that reads Maeterlinck and the public that accumulates money: the one largely feminine, the other largely masculine. Wholly incompatible in their ideals, they still pull together, as the ass and the ox must. But the ass shows no disposition to convert the ox, nor the ox the ass. They do not mitigate one another; they are, in biological phrase, infertile with one another.

But it happens that we have the rudiments of a middle tradition, a tradition that effectively combines theory and action, a tradition that is just as fundamentally American as either flag-waving or money-grabbing, one that is visibly growing but which has already been grossly abused; and this is the tradition that begins with Walt Whitman. The real significance of Whitman is that he, for the first time, gave us the sense of something organic in American life.

Whitman was himself a great vegetable of a man, all of a piece in roots, flavour, substantiality and succulence, well-ripened in the common sunshine. In him the hitherto incompatible extremes of the American temperament were fused. The refinement of the Puritan tradition, summed up as an original type in Jonathan Edwards, able to make noth-

ing of a life so rude in its actuality, turned for its outlet to a disembodied world, the shadow-world of Emerson, Hawthorne and Poe, a world fastidiously intellectual in which only two colours exist, white and black. Whitman was the Antæus of this tradition who touched earth with it and gave it hands and feet. For having all the ideas of New England being himself saturated with Emersonianism, he came up from the other side with everything New England did not possess: quantities of rude feeling and a faculty of gathering humane experience almost as great as that of the hero of the Odyssey. Living habitually among world ideas, world emotions, world impulses, and having experienced life on a truly grand scale, this extraordinary person, innocent as a pioneer of what is called urbanity, became nevertheless a man of the world in a sense in which ambassadors are not; and there is every reason to suppose that he would have been perfectly at home in the company of Achilles, or Erasmus, or Louis XIV.

This fact is full of meaning, and if any one doubts it let him dwell on the following record in Specimen Days. Whitman is describing what he did in the military hospitals at Washington during the war:

For reading I generally have some old pictorial magazines or story papers — they are always acceptable. . . . In these wards, or on the field, as I thus continue to go round, I have come to adapt myself to each emergency, after its kind or call, however trivial, however solemn, every one justified and made real under its circumstances — not only visits and cheering talk and little gifts — not only washing and dressing wounds . . . but passages from the Bible, expounding them, . . . etc. (I think I see my friends smiling at this confession, but I was never more in earnest in my life.) In camp and elsewhere, I was in the habit of reading or giving recitations to the men. They were very fond of it, and liked declamatory pieces. We would gather in a large group by ourselves after supper, and spend the time in such readings, or in talking, and occasionally by an amusing game called the game of twenty questions.

This passage will serve very well to mark the distinction between Whitman and all the other American men of letters of his time. Could Emerson have recited "declamatory pieces," even if it was at the moment the one thing to do? Could Bryant have led a game of twenty questions? Could Edgar Allan Poe have expounded the Bible? Could Whittier have juggled with oranges? Could Lowell have pointed out the felicities that lurk in the pictorial adventures of Nick Carter and the Wharf Rats? Could any one of them, in short, have entered so fully and many-sidedly into the spirit of a great human situation? But allowing for certain inevitable differences in the *milieu* (orange-juggling and the adventures of Nick Carter being peculiarly democratic and modern), I am sure that Achilles, or Erasmus, or Louis XIV could have done so; and this is why I have called Whitman a man of the world.

It was in these ways that he gained his experience, in these ways that he shared it. And it is the more remarkable since he had sprung from the most provincial, inadaptable, homespun stock, his aspect being, as Edmund Gosse remembered it, like that of a plain old deal table, scrubbed and scrubbed and scrubbed. He let in the air of a wider world on those inadequate decencies; he came home to his own traditions like a prodigal son, visiting for a while, mingling an element of indulgent pity in his new sense of the limited old ways, aware of a few confidences that could not be shared

any more and of so many things, human too, which could find no place there. To compare the particular homeliness of Whitman with the homeliness, for example, of Snow-Bound is at once to recall his line, "There was a child went forth."

And he challenged the abnormal dignity of American letters. The dignity of letters! No doubt in the perennial indignity of our world a considerable emphasis on that becomes all too easily the price of self-preservation. The possession of culture with us has always been rather a jealous possession, it has the nature of a right that has been earned, an investment that might have been a yacht, a country-house, or a collection of Rembrandts instead.

All this was especially true of the New York men of letters who formed the background of Whitman: Stedman, Stoddard, and their group, who cared so much for style, and for whom the essence of literature lay in its remoteness from Wall Street. They had the temperament of collectors and connoisseurs; and Whitman came in upon them thundering and with his coat off, like an inconvenient country uncle, puddling their artistic expectations. Could anything have been more disconcerting than his Olympian summary of what he calls the "endless supply of small coin . . . the dandies and ennuyees who flood us with their thin sentiment of parlours, parasols, piano-songs, tinkling rhymes, the five-hundredth importation — or whimpering and crying about something, chasing one aborted conceit after another," when, faced with this, he dwells only on a certain substantial grandeur in the mountains of white paper and the crashing presses that turn them out?

Whitman — how else can I express it? — precipitated the American character. All those things that had been separate, self-sufficient, incoordinate — action, theory, idealism, business — he cast into a crucible; and they emerged, harmonious and molten, in a fresh democratic ideal, based upon the whole personality. Every strong personal impulse, every cooperating and unifying impulse, everything that enriches the social background, everything that enriches the individual, everything that impels and clarifies in the modern world owes something to Whitman. And especially of those American writers who have written preeminently for young men — and which has not? — Whitman alone, it seems to me, has pitched his tone to the real spring of action in them.

All this indicates a function quite different from that of a poet in any but the most radical and primitive sense of the word (the sense in which it was held by Whitman himself), a man, that is to say, who first gives to a nation a certain focal centre in the consciousness of its own character. Virgil did this, Mazzini did this, Bjornson did this; and it was the main work of Whitman to make fast what he called "the idea and fact of American Totality," an idea and fact summed up with singular completeness in his own character and way of life. Emerson before him had provided a kind of skeleton outline; but what Emerson drew in black and white Whitman filled in with colour and set in three dimensions.

A focal centre — that is the first requisite of a great people. And by this I do not mean the sense of national or imperial destiny which has consolidated the great temporal powers of history. I mean that national "point of rest," to adopt a phrase in which Coleridge indicated that upon which the harmony of a work of art is founded and to which everything in the composition is more or less unconsciously referred; that secure and unobtrusive element of national character, taken for granted, and providing a certain underlying coherence and background of mutual understanding which Rome, for example, had in everything the name of Cato called up, or England in her great remembered worthies, or the elder Germany in Martin Luther. "National culture," to speak in the dialect of our own time, is only the perhaps too-conscious equivalent of this element in which everything admirably characteristic of a people sums itself up, which creates everywhere a kind of spiritual team-work, which radiates outward and articulates the entire living fabric of a race.

For us, it seems to me, Whitman laid the cornerstone of a national ideal capable in this way of releasing personality and of retrieving for our civilization, originally deficient in the richer juices of human nature, and still further bled and flattened out by the "machine process," the only sort of "place in the sun" that is really worth having.

But at this point one has to discriminate. The social ideal of Whitman is essentially a collection of raw materials, molten and malleable, which take shape only in an emotional form. This emotional attitude is at bottom the attitude of a perfectly free personality, naturally affirmative, naturally creative; the rude material of right personal instinct, which is, however, antecedent to the direction personality is to adopt and to the ideas that are to inform it.

To ignore this distinction, as most of the direct disciples of Whitman have done, is to go wrong utterly. And in fact Whitman himself ignored the distinction, and himself went wrong. Perfectly right in all his instinct, perfectly right so long as he kept to the plane of instinct, he was lost on the plane of ideas. He lacked a sure sense of his own province and limitations. Influenced no doubt by his disciples, he began in later years to assume functions not properly his own, and the greatness and sweetness of his character were increasingly marred by much pomposity and fatuousness. He was led to speak not as a poet but as an authority, the painful results of which may be seen in his newspaper interviews.

All this was probably inevitable. Whitman's instinct was to affirm everything, to accept everything, to relish the personal and human elements in everything. For himself he accepted "sustenance, clothing, shelter and continuity." As regards the world, he was equally catholic and passive. Soldiers being the strapping upright animals they are, he accepts armies because armies breed them. He enjoys an old restaurateur because he knows how to select champagne, likes to look at nursemaids because they are so trim and wholesome and fashionable women because they are so pretty and gay, likes money because of a certain strength it implies and business because it is so active, nimble and adventurous. On the plane of instinct, where he properly belongs, he is right in each case: on the plane of ideas, the practical effect is that, in accepting everything, he accepts the confusion of things and the *fait accompli.*

It is, in fact, the simple corollary of his thoroughgoing mood of affirmation on the personal, instinctive, emotional plane, that his ideas should be perfectly conventional. In ideas he is just an old-fashioned Jacksonian democrat. Except for a certain amount of uncommonly vigorous criticism, of the stock type, on American abuses, he never questions the old institutions. He takes for granted "the unform'd and nebulous state of

many things, not yet permanently settled, but agreed on all hands to be the preparations of an infinitely greater future." He talks the greatest amount of nonsense about the "feudalism" of a contemporary Europe whose typical artists have been men like Tolstoy, Dostoevski, Millet, Thomas Hardy. He is never able to release himself from the vicious comparative; he is morbid about geography. Not being satisfied by the greatness of anything as a positive fact, he has to prove its greatness by belittling something else. A fertile plain strikes him at once as more fertile than any other plain on earth, a grand scene "outvies all the historic places of note," an American general is more of a general than Napoleon, an American poem has to be better than any poem hitherto.

All this is just what Bryant used to say — it is just our fun. And the funniest thing of all, from this point of view, is to find Whitman solemnly posed, as he records it, before a vast canvas twenty feet by twelve, representing "Custer's Last Rally," the work of one John Mulvany; finding its "physiognomy realistic and Western," with an "almost entire absence of the stock traits of European war pictures," and recommending that it be sent to Paris "to show Messieur Crapeau [sic] that some things can be done in America as well as others." A scene that demonstrates once for all that Whitman was never intended to be an authority, even on democracy.

An opportunity, and in certain respects also a faculty, Whitman had, in his own time and place, very similar to those of Montaigne. I mean by this, on the one hand, a malleable and still incoherent race to be interpreted to itself, to be articulated, to be brought into focus, and on the other a temperament typical of that race, a range of sympathy coincidental with it, and a power of revealing and in a sense fixing the racial norm. "I look within myself, I am only concerned with myself, I reflect on myself, I examine myself, I take pleasure in myself," said Montaigne; and all France for the first time saw itself in a looking-glass and fell together in a common discipline.

The raw materials of a racial norm Whitman provided; but — and in this he resembled Emerson — he was too passive to go further. He assembled in himself and his writings the characteristics of America — with him originated the most contagious and most liberating, the most unifying of native impulses; but he failed to react upon them, to mould them, and to drive them home. He had no ideas, and he was satisfied to have none. He lacked, above all, intensity. He was too complacent. He was incapable of discipline and he did not see that discipline is, for Americans, the condition of all forward movement.

But the conventionality of Whitman's intellectual equipment is not, for us, a necessary part of the personal attitude which he originated. History is filled with instances of men who, having been called upon to originate fresh points of view, have had, in order to establish these points of view, to adopt a severely conventional position towards most of the phenomena of their time. Each of these men has had his disciples in the letter and his disciples in the spirit — Martin Luther, for example, especially in questions economic and social. The direct and immediate children of Luther, those who have laid apostolic hands on one another from generation to generation, are simply the bourgeoisie of the world; but the true Lutherans are those who, in every age, have thought keenly and honestly and independently and have, in so doing, contributed stone by stone to

the great catholicism of the future. So also with Whitman and the children of Whitman. It was inevitable, in the America of his time, that he should have been so much of an outrageous egoist (consider the provocation!), inevitable that he should, in Emerson's phrase, have swallowed the universe like a cake, inevitable that he should have been undiscriminating, confused and a little fatuous. To affirm sufficiently, he had to affirm everything.

We are in a different position, and we have different responsibilities. On the philosophical side, the simple doctrine of evolution, in its crude form the last word in Whitman's cosmos, has been refined and ripened. Above all, we have no excuse not to see that affirmation, in the most real sense, proceeds to a certain extent through rejection, by merely dropping off most of the old clothes that Whitman found quite good enough. To keep these old clothes, to affirm that since everything is good they must be good also, to embroider them and make them over and stalk about in them, loudly affirming one's own ego and the indiscriminate grandeur of all creation, with particular reference to the Whole Crowd of Good Americans — all this is not to continue and to reaffirm the right Whitmanian tradition; but it is, in a way, to have the sanction of Whitman's own character and experience, and it is, above all, to do what the typical contemporary Whitmanian does.

In some way — and primarily by returning upon Whitman as Whitman returned upon Emerson, not, as in that case, by adding emotion to intellect, but by adding intellect to emotion — the social ideal the raw materials of which have been provided by Whitman must be formulated and driven home.

D. H. Lawrence: WHITMAN, THE AMERICAN TEACHER

"There is a new voice in the old American classics," wrote D. H. Lawrence (1885–1930). "It is hard to hear a new voice, as hard as it is to listen to an unknown language." Of all the well-known English writers, Lawrence made the most serious, perceptive, and sympathetic study of American literature. He was particularly fond of Whitman. If the essay lacks total conviction, however, it is because Lawrence, who in many ways resembled Whitman, had mixed feelings about the poet.

Post mortem effects?

But what of Walt Whitman?
The "good grey poet."
Was he a ghost, with all his physicality?
The good grey poet.
Post mortem effects. Ghosts.
A certain ghoulish insistency. A certain horrible pottage of human parts. A certain stridency and portentousness. A luridness about his beatitudes.

DEMOCRACY! THESE STATES! EIDOLONS! LOVERS, ENDLESS LOVERS!

ONE IDENTITY!
ONE IDENTITY!
I AM HE THAT ACHES WITH AMOROUS LOVE.

Do you believe me, when I say post mortem effects?

When the *Pequod* went down, she left many a rank and dirty steamboat still fussing in the seas. The *Pequod* sinks with all her souls, but their bodies rise again to man innumerable tramp steamers, and ocean-crossing liners. Corpses.

What we mean is that people may go on, keep on, and rush on, without souls. They have their ego and their will, that is enough to keep them going.

So that you see, the sinking of the *Pequod* was only a metaphysical tragedy after all. The world goes on just the same. The ship of the *soul* is sunk. But the machine-manipulating body works just the same: digests, chews gum, admires Botticelli and aches with amorous love.

I AM HE THAT ACHES WITH AMOROUS LOVE.

What do you make of that? I AM HE THAT ACHES. First generalization. First uncomfortable universalization. WITH AMOROUS LOVE! Oh, God! Better a bellyache. A bellyache is at least specific. But the ACHE OF AMOROUS LOVE!

Think of having that under your skin. All that!

I AM HE THAT ACHES WITH AMOROUS LOVE.

Walter, leave off. You are not HE. You are just a limited Walter. And your ache doesn't include all Amorous Love, by any means. If you ache you only ache with a small bit of amorous love, and there's so much more stays outside the cover of your ache, that you might be a bit milder about it.

I AM HE THAT ACHES WITH AMOROUS LOVE.

CHUFF! CHUFF! CHUFF!

CHU-CHU-CHU-CHU-CHUFF!

Reminds one of a steam-engine. A locomotive. They're the only things that seem to me to ache with amorous love. All that steam inside them. Forty million foot-pounds pressure. The ache of AMOROUS LOVE. Steam-pressure. CHUFF!

An ordinary man aches with love for Belinda, or his Native Land, or the Ocean, or the Stars, or the Oversoul: if he feels that an ache is in the fashion.

It takes a steam-engine to ache with AMOROUS LOVE. All of it.

Walt was really too superhuman. The danger of the superman is that he is mechanical.

They talk of his "splendid animality." Well, he'd got it on the brain, if that's the place for animality.

I am he that aches with amorous love:
Does the earth gravitate, does not all
  matter, aching, attract all matter?
So the body of me to all I meet or know.

What can be more mechanical? The difference between life and matter is that life, living things, living creatures, have the instinct of turning right away from *some* matter, and of blissfully ignoring the bulk of most matter, and of turning towards only some certain bits of specially selected matter. As for living creatures all helplessly hurtling together into one great snowball, why, most very liv-ing creatures spend the greater part of their time getting out of the sight, smell or sound of the rest of living creatures. Even bees only cluster on their own queen. And that is sickening enough. Fancy all white humanity clustering on one another like a lump of bees.

No, Walt, you give yourself away. Matter *does* gravitate, helplessly. But men are tricky-tricksy, and they shy all sorts of ways.

Matter gravitates because it *is* helpless and mechanical.

And if you gravitate the same, if the body of you gravitates to all you meet or know, why, something must have gone seriously wrong with you. You must have broken your mainspring.

You must have fallen also into mechanization.

Your Moby Dick must be really dead. That lonely phallic monster of the individual you. Dead mentalized.

I only know that my body doesn't by any means gravitate to all I meet or know. I find I can shake hands with a few people. But most I wouldn't touch with a long prop.

Your mainspring is broken, Walt Whitman. The mainspring of your own individuality. And so you run down with a great whirr, merging with everything.

You have killed your isolate Moby Dick. You have mentalized your deep sensual body, and that's the death of it.

I am everything and everything is me and so we're all One in One Identity, like the Mundane Egg, which has been addled quite a while.

"Whoever you are, to endless announce-
  ments —"

"And of these one and all I weave the song of myself."

Do you? Well, then, it just shows you haven't *got* any self. It's a mush, not a woven thing. A hotch-potch, not a tissue. Your self.

Oh, Walter, Walter, what have you done with it? What have you done with yourself? With your own individual self? For it sounds as if it had all leaked out of you, leaked into the universe.

Post mortem effects. The individuality had leaked out of him.

No, no, don't lay this down to poetry. These are post mortem effects. And Walt's great poems are really huge fat tomb-plants, great rank graveyard growths.

All that false exuberance. All those lists of things boiled in one pudding-cloth! No, no!

I don't want all those things inside me, thank you.

"I reject nothing," says Walt.

If that is so, one must be a pipe organ at both ends, so everything runs through.

Post mortem effects.

"I embrace ALL," says Whitman. "I weave all things into myself."

Do you really! There can't be much left of *you* when you've done. When you've cooked the awful pudding of One Identity.

"And whoever walks a furlong without sympathy walks to his own funeral dressed in his own shroud."

Take off your hat then, my funeral procession of one is passing.

This awful Whitman. This post mor-
tem poet. This poet with the private soul leaking out of him all the time. All his privacy leaking out in a sort of dribble, oozing into the universe.

Walt becomes in his own person the whole world, the whole universe, the whole eternity of time. As far as his rather sketchy knowledge of history will carry him, that is. Because to *be* a thing he had to know it. In order to assume the identity of a thing, he had to know that thing. He was not able to assume one identity with Charlie Chaplin, for example, because Walt didn't know Charlie. What a pity! He'd have done poems, paeans and what not, Chants, Songs of Cinematernity.

"Oh, Charlie, my Charlie, another film is done — "

As soon as Walt *knew* a thing, he assumed a One Identity with it. If he knew that an Esquimo sat in a kyak, immediately there was Walt being little and yellow and greasy, sitting in a kyak.

Now will you tell me exactly what a kyak is?

Who is he that demands petty definition? Let him behold me *sitting in a kyak.*

I behold no such thing. I behold a rather fat old man full of a rather senile, self-conscious sensuosity.

DEMOCRACY. EN MASSE. ONE IDENTITY.

The universe, in short, adds up to ONE.

ONE.

1.

Which is Walt.

His poems, *Democracy, En Masse,*

One Identity, they are long sums in addition and multiplication, of which the answer is invariably MYSELF.

He reaches the state of ALLNESS.

And what then? It's all empty. Just an empty Allness. An addled egg.

Walt wasn't an esquimo. A little, yellow, sly, cunning, greasy little Esquimo. And when Walt blandly assumed Allness, including Esquimoness, unto himself, he was just sucking the wind out of a blown egg-shell, no more. Esquimos are not minor little Walts. They are something that I am not, I know that. Outside the egg of my Allness chuckles the greasy little Esquimo. Outside the egg of Whitman's Allness too.

But Walt wouldn't have it. He was everything and everything was in him. He drove an automobile with a very fierce headlight, along the track of a fixed idea, through the darkness of this world. And he saw Everything that way. Just as a motorist does in the night.

I, who happen to be asleep under the bushes in the dark, hoping a snake won't crawl into my neck; I, seeing Walt go by in his great fierce poetic machine, think to myself: What a funny world that fellow sees!

ONE DIRECTION! toots Walt in the car, whizzing along it.

Whereas there are myriads of ways in the dark, not to mention trackless wildernesses. As anyone will know who cares to come off the road, even the Open Road.

ONE DIRECTION! whoops America, and sets off also in an automobile.

ALLNESS! Shrieks Walt at a crossroad, going whizz over an unwary Red Indian.

ONE IDENTITY! chants democratic En Masse, pelting behind in motorcars, oblivious of the corpses under the wheels.

God save me, I feel like creeping down a rabbit-hole, to get away from all these automobiles rushing down the ONE IDENTITY track to the goal of ALLNESS.

"A woman waits for me — "

He might as well have said: "The femaleness waits for my maleness." Oh, beautiful generalization and abstraction! Oh, biological function.

"Athletic mothers of these States — " Muscles and wombs. They needn't have had faces at all.

"As I see myself reflected in Nature,
As I see through a mist, One with inexpressible completeness, sanity, beauty,
See the bent head, and arms folded over the breast, the Female I see."

Everything was female to him: even himself. Nature just one great function.

"This is the nucleus — after the child is born of woman, man is born of woman,
This is the bath of birth, the merge of small and large, and the outlet again — "

"The Female I see — "
If I'd been one of his women, I'd have given him Female. With a flea in his ear.
Always wanting to merge himself into the womb of something or other.
"The Female I see — "
Anything, so long as he could merge himself.
Just a horror. A sort of white flux.
Post mortem effects.
He found, like all men find, that you can't really merge in a woman, though you may go a long way. You can't man-

age the last bit. So you have to give it up, and try elsewhere. If you *insist* on merging.

In *Calamus* he changes his tune. He doesn't shout and thump and exult any more. He begins to hesitate, reluctant, wistful.

The strange calamus has its pink-tinged root by the pond, and it sends up its leaves of comradeship, comrades from one root, without the intervention of woman, the female.

So he sings of the mystery of manly love, the love of comrades. Over and over he says the same thing: the new world will be built on the love of comrades, the new great dynamic of life will be manly love. Out of this manly love will come the inspiration for the future.

Will it though? Will it?

Comradeship! Comrades! This is to be the new Democracy: of Comrades. This is the new cohering principle in the world: Comradeship.

Is it? Are you sure?

It is the cohering principle of true soldiery, we are told in *Drum Taps*. It is the cohering principle in the new unison for creative activity. And it is extreme and alone, touching the confines of death. Something terrible to bear, terrible to be responsible for. Even Walt Whitman felt it. The soul's last and most poignant responsibility, the responsibility of comradeship, of manly love.

"Yet you are beautiful to me, you faint-tinged roots, you make me think of death.
Death is beautiful from you (What indeed is finally beautiful except death and love?)
I think it is not for life I am chanting

here my chant of lovers, I think it must be for death,
For how calm, how solemn it grows to ascend to the atmosphere of lovers,
Death or life, I am then indifferent, my soul declines to prefer
(I am not sure but the high soul of lovers welcomes death most)
Indeed, O death, I think now these leaves mean precisely the same as you mean — "

This is strange, from the exultant Walt. Death!
Death is now his chant! Death!
Merging! And Death! Which is the final merge.
The great merge into the womb. Woman.
And after that, the merge of comrades: man-for-man love.

And almost immediately with this, death, the final merge of death.

There you have the progression of merging. For the great mergers, woman at last becomes inadequate. For those who love to extremes. Woman is inadequate for the last merging. So the next step is the merging of the man-for-man love. And this is on the brink of death. It slides over into death.

David and Jonathan. And the death of Jonathan.
It always slides into death.
The love of comrades.
Merging.
So that if the new Democracy is to be based on the love of comrades, it will be based on death too. It will slip so soon into death.

The last merging. The last Democracy.
The last love. The love of comrades.
Fatality. And fatality.

Whitman would not have been the

great poet he is if he had not taken the last steps and looked over into death. Death, the last merging, that was the goal of his manhood.

To the mergers, there remains the brief love of comrades, and then Death.

"Whereto answering, the sea
Delaying not, hurrying not
Whispered me through the night, very
   plainly before daybreak,
Lisp'd to me the low and delicious word
   death,
And again death, death, death, death.
Hissing melodions, neither like the bird
   nor like my arous'd child's heart,
But edging near as privately for me
   rustling at my feet,
Creeping thence steadily up to my ears
   and laving me softly all over
Death, death, death, death, death —"

Whitman is a very great poet, of the end of life. A very great post mortem poet, of the transitions of the soul as it loses its integrity. The poet of the soul's last shout and shriek, on the confines of death. *Après moi le déluge.*

But we have all got to die, and disintegrate.
We have got to die in life, too, and disintegrate while we live.
But even then the goal is not death. Something else will come.

"Out of the cradle endlessly rocking."

We've got to die first, anyhow. And disintegrate while we still live.

Only we know this much. Death is not the *goal.* And Love, and merging, are now only part of the death-process. Comradeship — part of the death-process. Democracy — part of death-process. The new Democracy — the brink of death. One Identity — death itself.

We have died, and we are still disintegrating.
But IT IS FINISHED.
Consummatum est.

Whitman, the great poet, has meant so much to me. Whitman, the one man breaking a way ahead. Whitman, the one pioneer. And only Whitman. No English pioneers, no French. No European pioneer-poets. In Europe the would-be pioneers are mere innovators. The same in America. Ahead of Whitman, nothing. Ahead of all poets, pioneering into the wilderness of unopened life, Whitman. Beyond him, none. His wide, strange camp at the end of the great high-road. And lots of new little poets camping on Whitman's camping ground now. But none going really beyond. Because Whitman's camp is at the end of the road, and on the edge of a great precipice. Over the precipice, blue distances, and the blue hollow of the future. But there is no way down. It is a dead end.

Pisgah. Pisgah sights. And Death. Whitman like a strange, modern, American Moses. Fearfully mistaken. And yet the great leader.

The essential function of art is moral. Not aesthetic, not decorative, not pastime and recreation. But moral. The essential function of art is moral.

But a passionate, implicit morality, not didactic. A morality which changes the blood, rather than the mind. Changes the blood first. The mind follows later, in the wake.

Now Whitman was a great moralist. He was a great leader. He was a great changer of the blood in the veins of men.

Surely it is especially true of American art, that it is all essentially moral. Hawthorne, Poe, Longfellow, Emerson, Melville: it is the moral issue which engages them. They all feel uneasy about the old morality. Sensuously, passionally, they all attack the old morality. But they know nothing better, mentally. Therefore they give tight mental allegiance to a morality which all their passion goes to destroy. Hence the duplicity which is the fatal flaw in them: most fatal in the most perfect American work of art, *The Scarlet Letter*. Tight mental allegiance given to a morality which the passional self repudiates.

Whitman was the first to break the mental allegiance. He was the first to smash the old moral conception, that the soul of man is something "superior" and "above" the flesh. Even Emerson still maintained this tiresome "superiority" of the soul. Even Melville could not get over it. Whitman was the first heroic seer to seize the soul by the scruff of her neck and plant her down among the potsherds.

"There!" he said to the soul. "Stay there!"

Stay there. Stay in the flesh. Stay in the limbs and lips and in the belly. Stay in the breast and womb. Stay there, O Soul, where you belong.

Stay in the dark limbs of negroes. Stay in the body of the prostitute. Stay in the sick flesh of the syphilitic. Stay in the marsh where the calamus grows. Stay there, Soul, where you belong.

The Open Road. The great home of the Soul is the open road. Not heaven, not paradise. Not "above." Not even "within." The soul is neither "above" nor "within." It is a wayfarer down the open road.

Not by meditating. Not by fasting. Not by exploring heaven after heaven, inwardly, in the manner of the great mystics. Not by exaltation. Not by ecstasy. Not by any of these ways does the soul come into her own.

Only by taking the open road.

Not through charity. Not through sacrifice. Not even through love. Not through good works. Not through these does the soul accomplish herself.

Only through the journey down the open road.

The journey itself, down the open road. Exposed to full contact. On two slow feet. Meeting whatever comes down the open road. In company with those that drift in the same measure along the same way. Towards no goal. Always the open road.

Having no known direction, even. Only the soul remaining true to herself in her going.

Meeting all the other wayfarers along the road. And how? How meet them, and how pass? With sympathy, says Whitman. Sympathy. He does not say love. He says sympathy. Feeling with. Feel with them as they feel with themselves. Catching the vibration of their soul and flesh as we pass.

It is a new great doctrine. A doctrine of life. A new great morality. A morality of actual living, not of salvation. Europe has never got beyond the morality of salvation. America to this day is deathly sick with saviourism. But Whitman, the greatest and the first and the only American teacher, was no Saviour. His morality was no morality of salvation. His was a morality of the soul living her life, not saving herself. Accepting the contact with other souls along the open way, as they lived their lives. Never trying to save them. As leave try to arrest them and throw them in gaol. The soul living her life along the incarnate mystery of the open road.

This was Whitman. And the true rhythm of the American continent speaking out in him. He is the first white aboriginal.

"In my Father's house are many mansions."

"No," said Whitman. "Keep out of mansions. A mansion may be heaven on earth, but you might as well be dead. Strictly avoid mansions. The soul is herself when she is going on foot down the open road."

It is the American heroic message. The soul is not to pile up defenses round herself. She is not to withdraw and seek her heavens inwardly, in mystical ecstasies. She is not to cry to some God beyond, for salvation. She is to go down the open road, as the road opens, into the unknown, keeping company with those whose soul draws them near to her, accomplishing nothing save the journey, and the works incident to the journey, in the long life-travel into the unknown, the soul in her subtle sympathies accomplishing herself by the way.

This is Whitman's essential message. The heroic message of the American future. It is the inspiration of thousands of Americans today, the best souls of today, men and women. And it is a message that only in America can be fully understood, finally accepted.

Then Whitman's mistake. The mistake of his interpretation of his watchword: Sympathy. The mystery of SYMPATHY. He still confounded it with Jesus' LOVE, and with Paul's CHARITY. Whitman, like all the rest of us, was at the end of

the great emotional highway of Love. And because he couldn't help himself, he carried on his Open Road as a prolongation of the emotional highway of Love, beyond Calvary. The highway of Love ends at the foot of the Cross. There is no beyond. It was a hopeless attempt, to prolong the highway of Love.

He didn't follow his Sympathy. Try as he might, he kept on automatically interpreting it as Love, as Charity. Merging.

This merging, en masse, One Identity, Myself monomania was a carry-over from the old Love idea. It was carrying the idea of Love to its logical physical conclusion. Like Flaubert and the leper. The decree of unqualified Charity, as the soul's one means of salvation, still in force.

Now Whitman wanted his soul to save itself, *he* didn't want to save it. Therefore he did not need the great Christian receipt for saving the soul. He needed to supersede the Christian Charity, the Christian Love, within himself, in order to give his Soul her last freedom. The highroad of Love is no Open Road. It is a narrow, tight way, where the soul walks hemmed in between compulsions.

Whitman wanted to take his Soul down the open road. And he failed in so far as he failed to get out of the old rut of Salvation. He forced his Soul to the edge of a cliff, and he looked down into death. And there he camped, powerless. He had carried out his Sympathy as an extension of Love and Charity. And it had brought him almost to madness and soul-death. It gave him his forced, unhealthy, post-mortem quality.

His message was really the opposite of Henley's rant:

I am the master of my fate.
I am the captain of my soul.

Whitman's essential message was the Open Road. The leaving of the soul free unto herself, the leaving of his fate to her and to the loom of the open road. Which is the bravest doctrine man has ever proposed to himself.

Alas, he didn't quite carry it out. He couldn't quite break the old maddening bond of the love-compulsion, he couldn't quite get out of the rut of the charity habit. For Love and Charity have degenerated now into habit: a bad habit.

Whitman said Sympathy. If only he had stuck to it! Because Sympathy means feeling with, not feeling for. He kept on having a passionate feeling *for* the negro slave, or the prostitute, or the syphilitic. Which is merging. A sinking of Walt Whitman's soul in the souls of these others.

He wasn't keeping to his open road. He was forcing his soul down an old rut. He wasn't leaving her free. He was forcing her into other peoples' circumstances.

Supposing he had felt true sympathy with the negro slave? He would have felt *with* the negro slave. Sympathy — compassion — which is partaking of the passion which was in the soul of the negro slave.

What was the feeling in the negro's soul?

"Ah, I am a slave! Ah, it is bad to be a slave! I must free myself. My soul will die unless she frees herself. My soul says I must free myself."

Whitman came along, and saw the slave, and said to himself: "That negro slave is a man like myself. We share the same identity. And he is bleeding with wounds. Oh, oh, is it not myself who am also bleeding with wounds?"

This was not *sympathy*. It was merging and self-sacrifice. "Bear ye one another's burdens." — "Love thy neighbour as thyself." — "Whatsoever ye do unto him, ye do unto me."

If Whitman had truly *sympathised*, he would have said: "That negro slave suffers from slavery. He wants to free himself. His soul wants to free him. He has wounds, but they are the price of freedom. The soul has a long journey from slavery to freedom. If I can help him I will: I will not take over his wounds and his slavery to myself. But I will help him fight the power that enslaves him when he wants to be free, if he wants my help. Since I see in his face that he needs to be free. But even when he is free, his soul has many journeys down the open road, before it is a free soul."

And of the prostitute Whitman would have said:

"Look at that prostitute! Her nature has turned evil under her mental lust for prostitution. She has lost her soul. She knows it herself. She likes to make men lose their souls. If she tried to make me lose my soul, I would kill her. I wish she may die."

But of another prostitute he would have said:

"Look! She is fascinated by the Priapic mysteries. Look, she will soon be worn to death by the Priapic usage. It is the way of her soul. She wishes it so."

Of the syphilitic he would say:

"Look! She wants to infect all men with syphilis. We ought to kill her."

And of another syphilitic:

"Look! She has a horror of her syphilis. If she looks my way I will help her to get cured."

This is sympathy. The soul judging for herself, and preserving her own integrity.

But when, in Flaubert, the man takes the leper to his naked body; when Bubi de Montparnasse takes the girl because he knows she's got syphilis; when Whitman embraces an evil prostitute: that is not sympathy. The evil prostitute has no desire to be embraced with love; so if you sympathise with her, you won't try to embrace her with love. The leper loathes his leprosy, so if you sympathise with him, you'll loathe it too. The evil woman who wishes to infect all men with her syphilis hates you if you haven't got syphilis. If you sympathise, you'll feel her hatred, and you'll hate too, you'll hate her. Her feeling is hate, and you'll share it. Only your soul will choose the direction of its own hatred.

The soul is a very perfect judge of her own motions, if your mind doesn't dictate to her. Because the mind says Charity! Charity! you don't have to force your soul into kissing lepers or embracing syphilitics. Your lips are the lips of your soul, your body is the body of your soul; your own single, individual soul. That is Whitman's message. And your soul hates syphilis and leprosy. Because it *is* a soul, it hates these things which are against the soul. And therefore to force the body of your soul into contact with uncleanness is a great violation of your soul. The soul wishes to keep clean and whole. The soul's deepest will is to preserve its own integrity, against the mind and the whole mass of disintegrating forces.

Soul sympathises with soul. And that which tries to kill my soul, my soul hates. My soul and my body are one. Soul and body wish to keep clean and whole. Only the mind is capable of great perversion. Only the mind tries to drive my soul and body into uncleanness and unwholesomeness.

What my soul loves, I love.

What my soul hates, I hate.

When my soul is stirred with compassion, I am compassionate.

What my soul turns away from, I turn away from.

That is the *true* interpretation of Whitman's creed: the true revelation of his Sympathy.

And my soul takes the open road. She meets the souls that are passing, she goes along with the souls that are going her way. And for one and all, she has sympathy. The sympathy of love, the sympathy of hate, the sympathy of simple proximity: all the subtle sympathisings of the incalculable soul, from the bitterest hate to the passionate love.

It is not I who guide my soul to heaven. It is I who am guided by my own soul along the open road, where all men tread. Therefore, I must accept her deep motions of love, or hate, or compassion, or dislike, or indifference. And I must go where she takes me. For my feet and my lips and my body are my soul. It is I who must submit to her.

This is Whitman's message of American democracy.

The true democracy, where soul meets soul, in the open road. Democracy. American democracy where all journey down the open road. And where a soul is known at once in its going. Not by its clothes or appearance. Whitman did away with that. Not by its family name. Not even by its reputation. Whitman and Melville both discounted that. Not by a progression of piety, or by works of Charity. Not by works at all. Not by anything but just itself. The soul passing unenhanced, passing on foot and being no more than itself. And recognized, and passed by or greeted according to the soul's dictate. If it be a great soul, it will be worshipped in the road.

The love of man and woman: a recognition of souls, and a communion of worship. The love of comrades: a recognition of souls, and a communion of worship. Democracy: a recognition of souls, all down the open road, and a great soul seen in its greatness, as it travels on foot among the rest, down the common way of the living. A glad recognition of souls, and a gladder worship of great and greater souls, because they are the only riches.

Love, and Merging, brought Whitman to the Edge of Death! Death! Death!

But the exultance of his message still remains. Purified of MERGING, purified of MYSELF, the exultant message of American Democracy, of souls in the Open Road, full of glad recognition, full of fierce readiness, full of joy of worship, when one soul sees a greater soul.

The only riches, the great souls.

Lobo, New Mexico

R. W. B. Lewis: THE NEW ADAM

In The American Adam (*1955*) *R. W. B. Lewis places Whitman's work in the nineteenth-century "dialogue" concerning the American character. In the dialogue it is generally agreed that the American is a "new man," an innocent or, as Emerson puts it, "the plain old Adam, the simple genuine self against the whole world." But the question is whether such a man, like the mythic hero of "Song of Myself," is really a hero or a menace — or both. Mr. Lewis teaches at Yale University.*

IN his old age, Dr. Holmes derived a certain amount of polite amusement from the poetry of Walt Whitman. Whitman, Holmes remarked, "carried the principle of republicanism through the whole world of created objects"; he smuggled into his "hospitable vocabulary words which no English dictionary recognizes as belonging to the language — words which will be looked for in vain outside of his own pages." Holmes found it hard to be sympathetic toward *Leaves of Grass;* it seemed to him windy, diffuse, and humorless; but his perceptions were as lively as ever. In these two observations he points to the important elements in Whitman which are central here: the spirit of equality which animated the surging catalogues of persons and things (on its more earthy level, not unlike Emerson's lists of poets and philosophers, with their equalizing and almost leveling tendency); the groping after novel words to identify novel experiences; the lust for inventiveness which motivated what was for Whitman the great act, the creative act.

Holmes's tone of voice, of course, added that for him Whitman had gone too far; Whitman was too original, too republican, too entire an Adam. Whitman had indeed gone further than

Holmes: a crucial and dimensional step further, as Holmes had gone further than Channing or Norton. In an age when the phrase "forward-looking" was a commonplace, individuals rarely nerved themselves to withstand the shock of others looking and moving even further forward than they. Emerson himself, who had gone so far that the liberal Harvard Divinity School forbade his presence there for more than thirty years, shared some of Holmes's feeling about Whitman. When his cordial letter welcoming *Leaves of Grass* in 1855 was published in the *New York Tribune,* Emerson muttered in some dismay that had he intended it for publication, he "should have enlarged the *but* very much — enlarged the *but.*" *Leaves of Grass* "was pitched in the very highest key of self-reliance," as a friend of its author maintained; but Emerson, who had given that phrase its contemporary resonance, believed that any attitude raised to its highest pitch tended to encroach dangerously on the truth of its opposite.

It would be no less accurate to say that Walt Whitman, instead of going too far forward, had gone too far backward: for he did go back, all the way back, to a primitive Adamic condition, to the beginning of time.

Reprinted from *The American Adam* by R. W. B. Lewis by permission of The University of Chicago Press, 1955. Copyright (1955) by The University of Chicago. Pages 41–53.

In the poetry of Walt Whitman, the hopes which had until now expressed themselves in terms of progress crystalized all at once in a complete recovery of the primal perfection. In the early poems Whitman accomplished the epochal return by huge and almost unconscious leaps. In later poems he worked his way more painstakingly up the river of history to its source: as, for example, in "Passage to India," where the poet moves back from the recently constructed Suez Canal, back past Christopher Columbus, past Alexander the Great and the most ancient of heroes and peoples, to the very "secret of the earth and sky." "In the beginning," John Locke once wrote, "all the world was America." Whitman manages to make us feel what it might have been like; and he succeeds at last in presenting the dream of the new Adam — along with his sorrows.

A measure of Whitman's achievement is the special difficulty which that dream had provided for others who tried to recount it. Its character was such that it was more readily described by those who did not wholly share in it. How can absolute novelty be communicated? All the history of the philosophy of language is involved with that question, from *The Cratylus* of Plato to the latest essay on semantics; and one could bring to bear on it the variety of anecdotes about Adam's naming the animals by the disturbingly simple device of calling a toad a toad.

Hawthorne conveyed the idea of novelty by setting it in an ancient pattern: allowing it thereby exactly to be *recognized;* and reaching a sharpness of meaning also to be found in Tocqueville's running dialectic of democracies and aristocracies. Whitman employed the same tactic when he said of Coleridge that he was "like Adam in Paradise, and just as free from artificiality." This was a more apt description of himself, as he knew:

I, chanter of Adamic songs,
Through the new garden the West, the great cities calling.

It is, in fact, in the poems gathered under the title *Children of Adam* (1860) that we have the most explicit evidence of his ambition to reach behind tradition to find and assert nature untroubled by art, to re-establish the natural unfallen man in the living hour. Unfallen man is, properly enough, unclothed as well; the convention of cover came in with the Fall; and Whitman adds his own unnostalgic sincerity to the Romantic affection for nakedness:

As Adam, early in the morning,
Walking forth from the bower refresh'd with sleep,
Behold me where I pass, hear my voice, approach,
Touch me, touch the palm of your hand to my body as I pass,
Be not afraid of my body.

For Whitman, as for Holmes and Thoreau, the quickest way of framing his novel outlook was by lowering, and secularizing, the familiar spiritual phrases: less impudently than Thoreau but more earnestly, and indeed more monotonously, but with the same intention of salvaging the human from the religious vocabulary to which (he felt) it had given rise. Many of Whitman's poetic statements are conversions of religious allusion: the new miracles were acts of the senses (an odd foreshortening, incidentally, of Edwards' Calvinist elaboration of the Lockian psychology); the aroma of the body was "finer than prayer"; his head was "more than churches, bibles and all creeds." "If I worship one thing more than another," Whitman declaimed, in a moment of Adamic narcissism, "it shall be the spread of my own body." These assertions gave a peculiar stress to Whitman's seconding of the hopeful belief in men like gods: "Divine am I, inside and out, and I make holy whatever I touch." Whitman's poetry is at every moment an act of turbulent incarnation.

But although there is, as there was meant to be, a kind of shock-value in such lines, they are not the most authentic index to his pervasive Adamism, because in them the symbols have become too explicit and so fail to work symbolically. Whitman in these instances is stating his position and contemplating it; he is betraying his own principle of indirect statement; he is telling us too much, and the more he tells us, the more we seem to detect the anxious, inflated utterance of a charlatan. We cling to our own integrity and will not be thundered at. We respond far less willingly to Whitman's frontal assaults than we do to his dramatizations; when he is enacting his role rather than insisting on it, we are open to persuasion. And he had been enacting it from the outset of *Leaves of Grass*.

This is the true nature of his achievement and the source of his claim to be the representative poet of the party of Hope. For the "self" in the very earliest of Whitman's poems is an individual who is always moving forward. To say so is not merely to repeat that Whitman believed in progress; indeed, it is in some sense to deny it. The young Whitman, at least, was not an apostle of progress in its customary meaning of a motion from worse to better to best, an improvement over a previous historic condition, a "rise of man." For Whitman, there was

no past or "worse" to progress from; he moved forward because it was the only direction (he makes us think) in which he could move; because there was nothing behind him — or if there were, he had not yet noticed it. There is scarcely a poem of Whitman's before, say, 1867, which does not have the air of being the first poem ever written, the first formulation in language of the nature of persons and of things and of the relations between them; and the urgency of the language suggests that it was formulated in the very nick of time, to give the objects described their first substantial existence.

Nor is there, in *Leaves of Grass*, any complaint about the weight or intrusion of the past; in Whitman's view the past had been so effectively burned away that it had, for every practical purpose, been forgotten altogether. In his own recurring figure, the past was already a corpse; it was on its way out the door to the cemetery; Whitman watched it absentmindedly, and turned at once to the living reality. He did enjoy, as he reminds us, reciting Homer while walking beside the ocean; but this was just because Homer was exempt from tradition and talking at and about the dawn of time. Homer was the poet you found if you went back far enough; and as for the sea, it had (unlike Melville's) no sharks in it — no ancient, lurking, indestructible evil powers. Whitman's hope was unspoiled by memory. When he became angry, as he did in *Democratic Vistas* (1871), he was not attacking his generation in the Holgrave manner for continuing to accept the old and the foreign, but for fumbling its extraordinary opportunity, for taking a wrong turn on the bright new highway he had mapped for it. Most of the time he was more interested in the map, and we are more interested in him when he was.

It was then that he caught up and set to music the large contemporary conviction that man had been born anew in the new society, that the race was off to a fresh start in America. It was in *Leaves of Grass*, that the optative mood, which had endured for over a quarter of a century and had expressed itself so variously and so frequently, seemed to have been transformed at last into the indicative. It was there that the hope that had enlivened spokesmen from Noah Webster in 1825 ("American glory begins at the dawn") to the well-named periodical, *Spirit of the Age* in 1849 ("The accumulated atmosphere of ages, containing stale ideas and opinions . . . will soon be among the things that were") — that all that stored-up abundance of hope found its full poetic realization. *Leaves of Grass* was a climax as well as a beginning, or rather, it was the climax of a long effort to begin.

This was why Emerson, with whatever enlarged "buts" in his mind, made a point of visiting Whitman in New York and Boston; why Thoreau, refusing to be put off "by any brag or egoism in his book," preferred Whitman to Bronson Alcott; and why Whitman, to the steady surprise of his countrymen, has been regarded in Europe for almost a century as unquestionably the greatest poet the New World has produced: an estimate which even Henry James would come round to. European readers were not slow to recognize in Whitman an authentic rendering of their own fondest hopes; for if much of his vision had been originally imported from Germany and France, it had plainly lost its portion of nostalgia en route. While European romanticism continued to resent the effect of time, Whitman was announcing that time had only just begun. He was able to think so because of the facts of immediate history in America during the years when he was maturing: when a world was, in some literal way, being created before his eyes. It was this that Whitman had the opportunity to dramatize; and it was this that gave *Leaves of Grass* its special quality of a Yankee Genesis: a new account of the creation of the world — the creation, that is, of a new world; an account this time with a happy ending for Adam its hero; or better yet, with no ending at all; and with this important emendation, that now the creature has taken on the role of creator.

It was a twofold achievement, and the second half of it was demanded by the first. We see the sequence, for example, in the development from section 4 to section 5 of "Song of Myself." The first phase was the identification of self, an act which proceeded by distinction and differentiation, separating the self from every element that in a traditional view might be supposed to be part of it: Whitman's identity card had no space on it for the names of his ancestry. The exalted mind which carried with it a conviction of absolute novelty has been described by Whitman's friend, the Canadian psychologist, Dr. R. M. Bucke, who relates it to what he calls Whitman's "cosmic consciousness." "Along with the consciousness of the cosmos [Dr. Bucke wrote], there occurs an intellectual enlightenment which alone would place the individual on a new plane of existence — would make him almost a member of a new species." *Almost a member of a new species:* that could pass as the slogan of each individual in the party of Hope. It was a robust American effort to make real and operative the condition which John Donne once had merely feared:

Prince, Subject, Father, Son are things forgot,
For every man alone thinks he has got

To be a Phoenix and that then can be
None of that kind, of which he is, but he.

Whitman achieves the freedom of the
new condition by scrupulously peeling
off every possible source of, or influence
upon, the "Me myself," the "what I am."
As in section 4 of "Song of Myself":

Trippers and askers surround me
People I meet, the effect upon me of my
    early life, or the ward and the city I live
    in or the nation. . . .
The sickness of one of my folks, or of myself,
    or the ill-doing or loss or lack of money,
    or depressions or exaltations,
Battles, the horror of fratricidal wars, the
    fever of doubtful news, the fitful events,
These come to me days and nights and go
    from me again,
But they are not the Me myself.
Apart from the pulling and hauling stands
    what I am;
Stands amused, complacent, compassionat-
    ing, idle, unitary;
Looks down, is erect, or bends an arm on an
    impalpable certain rest,
Looking with side-curved head curious what
    will come next,
Both in and out of the game, and watching
    and wondering at it.

There is Emerson's individual, the "infinitely repellent orb." There is also the
heroic product of romanticism, exposing
behind the mass of what were regarded
as inherited or external or imposed and
hence superficial and accidental qualities
the true indestructible secret core of personality. There is the man who contends
that "nothing, not God, is greater to one
than one's self."

There, in fact, is the new Adam. If we
want a profile of him, we could start
with the adjectives Whitman supplies:
amused, complacent, compassionating,
idle, unitary; especially unitary, and certainly very easily amused; too compla-

cent, we frequently feel, but always compassionate — expressing the old divine
compassion for every sparrow that falls,
every criminal and prostitute and hopeless invalid, every victim of violence or
misfortune. With Whitman's help we
could pile up further attributes, and the
exhaustive portrait of Adam would be
composed of a careful gloss on each one
of them: hankering, gross, mystical,
nude; turbulent, fleshy, sensual, eating,
drinking, and breeding; no sentimentalist, no stander above men and women;
no more modest than immodest; wearing
his hat as he pleases indoors and out;
never skulking or ducking or deprecating; adoring himself and adoring his
comrades; afoot with his vision,

Moving forward then and now and forever,
Gathering and showing more always and
    with velocity,
Infinite and omnigenous.

And announcing himself in language like
that. For an actual illustration, we could
not find anything better than the stylized
daguerreo-type of himself which Whitman placed as the Frontispiece of the
first edition. We recognize him at once:
looking with side-curved head, bending
an arm on the certain rest of his hip, evi-
dently amused, complacent, and curious;
bearded, rough, probably sensual; with
his hat on.

Whitman did resemble this Adamic
archetype, according to his friend John
Burroughs. "There was a look about
him," Burroughs remembered, "hard to
describe, and which I have seen in no
other face, — a gray, brooding, elemental
look, like the granite rock, something
primitive and Adamic that might have
belonged to the first man." The two new
adjectives there are "gray" and "brooding"; and they belong to the profile, too,

both of Whitman and of the character he dramatized. There was bound to be some measure of speculative sadness inherent in the situation. Not all the leaves Whitman uttered were joyous ones, though he wanted them all to be and was never clear why they were not. His ideal image of himself — and it is his best single trope for the new Adam — was that of a live oak he saw growing in Louisiana:

All alone stood it and the mosses hung down
  from the branches,
Without any companion it grew there uttering joyous leaves of dark green,
And its look, rude, unbending, lusty, made
  me think of myself.

But at his most honest, he admitted, as he does here, that the condition was somehow unbearable:

I wondered how it could utter joyous leaves
  standing alone there without a friend near,
  for I knew I could not . . . .
And though the live-oak glistens there in
  Louisiana solitary in a wide flat space,
Uttering joyous leaves all its life without a
  friend a lover near,
I knew very well I could not.

Adam had his moments of sorrow also. But the emotion had nothing to do with the tragic insight; it did not spring from any perception of a genuine hostility in nature or lead to the drama of colliding forces. Whitman was wistful, not tragic. We might almost say that he was wistful because he was not tragic. He was innocence personified. It is not difficult to marshal a vast array of references to the ugly, the gory, and the sordid in his verses; brought together in one horrid lump, they appear as the expression of one who was well informed about the shabby side of the world; but though he offered himself as "the poet of wicked-

ness" and claimed to be "he who knew what it was to be evil," every item he introduced as vile turns out, after all, to be merely a particular beauty of a different original coloration. "Evil propels me and reform of evil propels me, I stand indifferent." A sentiment like that can make sense only if the term "evil" has been filtered through a transfiguring moral imagination, changing in essence as it passes.

That sentiment, of course, is not less an expression of poetic than of moral motivation. As a statement of the poetic sensibility, it could have been uttered as easily by Shakespeare or Dante as by Whitman. Many of the very greatest writers suggest, as Whitman does, a peculiar artistic innocence, a preadolescent wonder which permits such a poet to take in and reproject whatever there is, shrinking from none of it. But in Whitman, artistic innocence merged with moral innocence: a preadolescent ignorance of the convulsive undertow of human behavior — something not at all shared by Dante or Shakespeare. Both modes of innocence are present in the poetry of Walt Whitman, and they are not at any time to be really distinguished. One can talk about his image of moral innocence only in terms of his poetic creation.

"I reject none, accept all, then reproduce all in my own forms." The whole spirit of Whitman is in the line: there is his strategy for overcoming his sadness, and the second large phase of his achievement, following the act of differentiation and self-identification. It is the creative phase, in that sense of creativity which beguiles the artist most perilously into stretching his analogy with God — when he brings a world into being. Every great poet composes a world for us, and what James called the "figure in the carpet" is the poet's private chart of that world; but when we speak of the poet's world — of Dostoevski's or Balzac's — we knowingly skip a phrase, since what we mean is Dostoevski's (or Balzac's) selective embodiment of an already existing world. In the case of Whitman, the type of extreme Adamic romantic, the metaphor gains its power from a proximity to the literal, as though Whitman really were engaged in the stupendous task of building a world that had not been there before the first words of his poem.

The task was self-imposed, for Whitman's dominant emotion, when it was not unmodified joy, was simple, elemental loneliness; it was a testimony to his success and contributed to his peculiar glow. For if the hero of *Leaves of Grass* radiates a kind of primal innocence in an innocent world, it was not only because he had made that world, it was also because he had begun by making himself. Whitman is an early example, and perhaps the most striking one we have, of the self-made man, with an undeniable grandeur which is the product of his manifest sense of having been responsible for his own being — something far more compelling than the more vulgar version of the rugged individual who claims responsibility only for his own bank account.

And of course he was lonely, incomparably lonely; no anchorite was ever so lonely, since no anchorite was ever so alone. Whitman's image of the evergreen, "solitary in a wide, flat space . . . without a friend a lover near," introduced what more and more appears to be the central theme of American literature, in so far as a unique theme may be claimed for it: the theme of loneliness, dramatized in what I shall later describe as the story of *the hero in space.* The only recourse for a poet like Whit-

man was to fill the space by erecting a home and populating it with companions and lovers.

Whitman began in an Adamic condition which was only too effectively realized: the isolated individual, standing flush with the empty universe, a primitive moral and intellectual entity. In the behavior of a "noiseless, patient spider," Whitman found a revealing analogy:

A noiseless, patient spider
I mark'd where, on a little promontory, it
   stood out, isolated,
Mark'd how, to explore the vacant, vast
   surrounding,
It launched forth filament, filament, filament,
   out of itself,
Ever unreeling them — ever tirelessly speeding them.

"Out of itself." This is the reverse of the traditionalist attitude that, in Eliot's phrase, "home is where one starts from." Whitman acted on the hopeful conviction that the new Adam started from himself; having created himself, he must next create a home. The given in individual experience was no longer a complex of human, racial, and familial relationships; it was a self in a vacant, vast surrounding. Each simple separate person must forge his own framework anew. This was the bold, enormous venture inevitably confronted by the Adamic personality. He had to become the maker of his own conditions — if he were to have any conditions or any achieved personality at all.

There were, in any case, no conditions to *go back to* — to take upon one's self or to embody. There is in fact almost no indication at all in *Leaves of Grass* of a return or reversion, even of that recovery of childhood detected in *Walden.* Whitman begins after that recovery, as a child, seemingly self-propagated, and he is always going *forth;* one of his pleasantest poems was constructed around that figure. There is only the open road, and Whitman moves forward from the start of it. Homecoming is for the exile, the prodigal son, Adam after the expulsion, not for the new unfallen Adam in the western garden. Not even in "Passage to India" is there a note of exile, because there is no sense of sin ("Let others weep for sin"). Whitman was entirely remote from the view of man as an orphan which motivated many of the stories of Hawthorne and Melville and which underlay the characteristic adventure they narrated of the search for a father. Hawthorne, an orphan himself and the author of a book about England called *Our Old Home,* sometimes sent his heroes to Europe to look for their families; Melville dispatched his heroes to the bottom of the sea on the same mission. This was the old way of posing the problem: the way of mastering life by the recovery of home, though it might require descent to the land of the dead; but Whitman knew the secret of his paternity.

Whitman was creating a world, even though he often sounds as though he were saluting a world that had been lying in wait for him: "Salut au monde." In one sense, he is doing just that, welcoming it, acknowledging it, reveling in its splendor and variety. His typical condition is one of acceptance and absorption; the word which almost everyone who knew him applied to his distinguishing capacity was "absorptive." He absorbed life for years; and when he contained enough, he let it go out from him again. "I . . . accept all, then reproduce all in my own forms." He takes unflagging delight in the reproductions: "Me pleased," he says in "Our Old Feuillage"; it is the "what I am." But the pleasure of seeing becomes actual only in the process of naming. It is hard to recall any particular of life and work, of men and women and animals and plants and things, of body and mind, that Whitman has not somewhere named in caressing detail. And the process of naming is for Whitman nothing less than the process of creation. This new Adam is both maker and namer; his innocent pleasure, untouched by humility, is colored by the pride of one who looks on his work and finds it good. The things that are named seem to spring into being at the sound of the word. It was through the poetic act that Whitman articulated the dominant metaphysical illusion of his day and became the creator of his own world.

We have become familiar, a century after the first edition of *Leaves of Grass,* with the notion of the poet as the magician who "orders reality" by his use of language. That notion derived originally from the epochal change — wrought chiefly by Kant and Hegel — in the relation between the human mind and the external world; a change whereby the mind "thought order into" the sensuous mass outside it instead of detecting an order externally existing. Whitman (who read Hegel and who wrote a singularly flatulent poetic reflection after doing so) adapted that principle to artistic creativity with a vigor and enthusiasm unknown before James Joyce and his associates in the twentieth century. What is implicit in every line of Whitman is the belief that the poet *projects* a world of order and meaning and identity into either a chaos or a sheer vacuum; he does not *discover* it. The poet may salute the chaos; but he creates the world.

Such a conviction contributed greatly to Whitman's ever enlarging idea of the poet as the vicar of God, as the son of God — as God himself. Those were not new labels for the artist, but they had been given fresh currency in Whitman's generation; and Whitman held to all of them more ingenuously than any other poet who ever lived. He supervised the departure of "the priests" and the arrival of the new vicar, "the divine litteratus"; he erected what he called his novel "trinitas" on the base of "the true son of God, the poet"; he offered himself as a cheerful, divine scapegoat and stage-managed "my own crucifixion." And to the extent that he fulfilled his own demands for *the* poet — as laid down in the Preface to *Leaves of Grass* and in *Democratic Vistas* — Whitman became God the Creator.

This was the mystical side of him, the side which announced itself in the fifth section of "Song of Myself," and which led to the mystical vision of a newly created totality. The vision emerges from those lyrical sweeps through the universe in the later sections of the poem: the sections in which Whitman populated and gave richness and shape to the universe by the gift of a million names. We can round out our picture of Whitman as Adam — both Adam as innocent and Adam as namer — if we distinguish his own brand of mysticism from the traditional variety. Traditional mysticism proceeds by denial and negation and culminates in the imagery of deserts and silence, where the voice and the being of God are the whole of reality. Whitman's mysticism proceeds by expansive affirmation and culminates in plenitude and huge volumes of noise. Traditional mysticism is the surrender of the ego to its creator, in an eventual escape from the limits of names; Whitman's is the expansion of the ego in the act of creation itself, naming every conceivable object as it comes from the womb.

The latter figure is justified by the very numerous references, both by Whitman and by his friends, to his "great mother-nature." We must cope with the remarkable blend in the man, whereby this Adam, who had already grown to the stature of his own maker, was not less and at the same time his own Eve, breeding the human race out of his love affair with himself. If section 5 of "Song of Myself" means anything, it means this: a miraculous intercourse between "you my soul" and "the other I am," with a world as its offspring. How the process worked in his poems can be seen by examining any one of the best of them. There Whitman skilfully brings into being the small world of the particular poem by introducing a few items one by one, linking them together by a variety of devices, running back over them time and again to reinsure their solidity and durability, adding further items and quickly forging the relations between them and the cluster already present, announcing at the end the accomplished whole and breathing over all of it the magical command *to be.*

Take, for example, "Crossing Brooklyn Ferry":

Flood-tide below me! I see you face to face!
Clouds of the west — sun there half an hour high — I see you also face to face.
Crowds of men and women attired in the usual costumes, how curious you are to me!
On the ferry-boats the hundreds and hundreds that cross, returning home, are more curious to me than you suppose,
And you that shall cross from shore to shore years hence are more to me, and more in my meditations, than you might suppose.

This is not the song of a *trovatore*, a finder, exposing bit by bit the substance of a spectacle which is there before a spectator looks at it. It is the song of a poet who creates his spectacle by "projecting" it as he goes along. The flood tides, the clouds, the sun, the crowds of men and women in the usual costumes: these exist in the instant they are named and as they are pulled in toward one another, bound together by a single unifying eye through the phrases which apply to them severally ("face to face," "curious to me"). The growth of the world is exactly indicated in the increasing length of the lines; until, in the following stanza, Whitman can observe a "simple, compact, well-join'd scheme." Stabilized in space, the scheme must now be given stabilizing relations in time; Whitman goes on to announce that "fifty years hence, others will see them as they cross, the sun half an hour high" (the phrase had to be repeated) "a hundred years hence, or ever so many hundred years hence, others will see them." With the world, so to speak, a going concern, Whitman is able now to summon new elements into existence: sea gulls, the sunlight in the water, the haze on the hills, the schooners and sloops and ships at anchor, the large and small steamers, and the flags of all nations. A few of the conspicuous elements are blessed and praised, in an announcement (stanza 8) not only of their existence but now rather of the value they impart to one another; and then, in the uninterrupted prayer of the final stanza (stanza 9 — the process covers nine stanzas, as though it were nine months) each separate entity is named again as receiving everlasting life through its participation in the whole:

Flow on river! flow with the flood-tide, and
    ebb with the ebb-tide!
Frolic on, crested and scallop-edg'd waves!

And so on: until the mystery of incarnation has been completed.

Randall Jarrell: SOME LINES FROM WHITMAN

Randall Jarrell is a poet, critic, and teacher who resists current orthodoxies. His reasons for admiring Whitman are opposed to the prevailing taste for painstaking formal refinement in poetry. Indeed Jarrell admires Whitman for the very "barbarism" that Santayana deplores. To make up one's mind about Whitman in the presence of Jarrell and Santayana is a severe test of literary taste and judgment.

WHITMAN, Dickinson, and Melville seem to me the best poets of the 19th Century here in America. Melville's poetry has been grotesquely underestimated, but of course it is only in the last four or five years that it has been much read; in the long run, in spite of the awkwardness and amateurishness of so much of it, it will surely be thought well of. (In the short run it will probably be thought entirely too well of. Melville is a great poet only in the prose of *Moby Dick*.) Dickinson's poetry has been thoroughly read, and well though undifferentiatingly loved — after a few decades or centuries almost everybody will be able to see through Dickinson to her poems. But something odd has happened to the living changing part of Whitman's reputation: nowadays it is people who are not particularly interested in poetry, people who say that they read a poem for what it says, not for how it says it, who admire Whitman most. Whitman is often written about, either approvingly or disapprovingly, as if he were the Thomas Wolfe of 19th Century democracy, the hero of a de Mille movie about Walt Whitman. (People even talk about a war in which Walt Whitman and Henry James chose up sides, to begin with, and in which you and I will go on fighting till the day we die.) All this sort of thing,

and all the bad poetry that there of course is in Whitman — for any poet has written enough bad poetry to scare away anybody — has helped to scare away from Whitman most "serious readers of modern poetry." They do not talk of his poems, as a rule, with any real liking or knowledge. Serious readers, people who are ashamed of not knowing all Hopkins by heart, are not at all ashamed to say, "I don't really know Whitman very well." This may harm Whitman in your eyes, they know, but that is a chance that poets have to take. Yet "their" Hopkins, that good critic and great poet, wrote about Whitman, after seeing five or six of his poems in a newspaper review: "I may as well say what I should not otherwise have said, that I always knew in my heart Walt Whitman's mind to be more like my own than any other man's living. As he is a very great scoundrel this is not a very pleasant confession." And Henry James, the leader of "their" side in that awful imaginary war of which I spoke, once read Whitman to Edith Wharton (much as Mozart used to imitate, on the piano, the organ) with such power and solemnity that both sat shaken and silent; it was after this reading that James expressed his regret at Whitman's "too extensive acquaintance with the foreign languages." Almost all the most "original and advanced" poets and critics and readers of the last part of the 19th Century thought Whitman as original and advanced as themselves, in manner as well as in matter. Can Whitman really be a sort of Thomas Wolfe or Carl Sandburg or Robinson Jeffers or Henry Miller — or a sort of Balzac of poetry, whose every part is crude but whose whole is somehow great? He is not, nor could he be; a poem, like Pope's spider, "lives along the line," and all the dead lines in the world will not make one live poem. As Blake says, "all sublimity is founded on minute discrimination," and it is in these "minute particulars" of Blake's that any poem has its primary existence.

To show Whitman for what he is one does not need to praise or explain or argue, one needs simply to quote. He himself said, "I and mine do not convince by arguments, similes, rhymes,/ We convince by our presence." Even a few of his phrases are enough to show us that Whitman was no sweeping rhetorician, but a poet of the greatest and oddest delicacy and originality and sensitivity, so far as words are concerned. This is, after all, the poet who said, "Blind loving wrestling touch, sheath'd hooded sharp-tooth'd touch"; who said, "Smartly attired, countenance smiling, form upright, death under the breast-bones, hell under the skull-bones"; who said, "Agonies are one of my changes of garments"; who saw grass as the "flag of my disposition," saw "the sharp-peak'd farmhouse, with its scallop'd scum and slender shoots from the gutters," heard a plane's "wild ascending lisp," and saw and heard how at the amputation "what is removed drops horribly in a pail." This is the poet for whom the sea was "howler and scooper of storms," reaching out to us with "crooked inviting fingers"; who

went "leaping chasms with a pike-pointed staff, clinging to topples of brittle and blue"; who, a runaway slave, saw how "my gore dribs, thinn'd with the ooze of my skin"; who went "lithographing Kronos . . . buying drafts of Osiris"; who stared out at the "little plentiful mannikins skipping around in collars and tail'd coat,/ I am aware who they are, (they are positively not worms or fleas)." For he is, at his best, beautifully witty: he says gravely, "I find I incorporate gneiss, coals, long-threaded moss, fruits, grain, esculent roots,/ And am stucco'd with quadrupeds and birds all over"; and of these quadrupeds and birds "not one is respectable or unhappy over the whole earth." He calls advice: "Unscrew the locks from the doors! Unscrew the doors from their jambs!" He publishes the results of research: "Having pried through the strata, analyz'd to a hair, counsel'd with doctors and calculated close,/ I find no sweeter fat than sticks to my own bones." Everybody remembers how he told the Muse to "cross out please those immensely overpaid accounts,/ That matter of Troy and Achilles' wrath, and Aeneas', Odysseus' wanderings," but his account of the arrival of the "illustrious emigré" here in the New World is even better: "Bluff'd not a bit by drainpipe, gasometer, artificial fertilizers,/ Smiling and pleas'd with palpable intent to stay,/ She's here, install'd amid the kitchenware." Or he sees, like another Breughel, "the mechanic's wife with the babe at her nipple interceding for every person born,/ Three scythes at harvest whizzing in a row from three lusty angels with shirts bagg'd out at their waists,/ The snag-toothed hostler with red hair redeeming sins past and to come" — the passage has enough wit not only (in Johnson's phrase) to keep it sweet, but enough to make it believable. He says:

I project my hat, sit shame-faced, and beg.

Enough! Enough! Enough!
Somehow I have been stunn'd. Stand back!
Give me a little time beyond my cuff'd head,
    slumbers, dreams, gaping,
I discover myself on the verge of a usual
    mistake.

There is in such changes of tone as these the essence of wit. And Whitman is even more far-fetched than he is witty; he can say about Doubters, in the most improbable and explosive of juxtapositions: "I know every one of you, I know the sea of torment, doubt, despair and unbelief./ How the flukes splash! How they contort rapid as lightning, with splashes and spouts of blood!" Who else would have said about God: "As the hugging and loving bed-fellow sleeps at my side through the night, and withdraws at the break of day with stealthy tread,/ Leaving me baskets cover'd with white towels, swelling the house with their plenty"? — the Psalmist himself, his cup running over, would have looked at Whitman with dazzled eyes. (Whitman was persuaded by friends to hide the fact that it was God he was talking about.) He says, "Flaunt of the sunshine I need not your bask — lie over!" This unusual employment of verbs is usual enough in participle-loving Whitman, who also asks you to "look in my face while I snuff the sidle of evening," or tells you, "I effuse my flesh in eddies, and drift it in lacy jags." Here are some typical beginnings of poems: "City of orgies, walks, and joys. . . . Not heaving from my ribb'd breast only. . . . O take my hand Walt Whitman! Such gliding wonders! Such sights and sounds! Such join'd unended links. . . ." He says to the objects of the world, "You have waited, you always wait, you dumb, beautiful ministers"; sees "the sun and stars that float in the open air,/ The apple-shaped earth"; says, "O suns — O grass of graves — O perpetual transfers and promotions,/ If you do not say anything how can I say anything?" Not many poets have written better, in queerer and more convincing and more individual language, about the world's *gliding wonders:* the phrase seems particularly right for Whitman. He speaks of those "circling rivers the breath," of the "savage old mother incessantly crying,/ To the boy's soul's questions sullenly timing, some drown'd secret hissing" — ends a poem, once, "We have voided all but freedom and our own joy." How can one quote enough? If the reader thinks that all this is like Thomas Wolfe he *is* Thomas Wolfe; nothing else could explain it. Poetry like this is as far as possible from the work of any ordinary rhetorician, whose phrases cascade over us like suds of the oldest and most-advertised detergent.

The interesting thing about Whitman's worst language (for, just as few poets have ever written better, few poets have ever written worse) is how unusually absurd, how really ingeniously bad, such language is. I will quote none of the most famous examples; but even a line like *O culpable! I acknowledge. I exposé!* is not anything that you and I could do — only a man with the most extraordinary feel for language, or none whatsoever, could have cooked up Whitman's worst messes. For instance: what other man in all the history of this planet would have said, "I am a habitan of Vienna"? (One has an immediate vision of him as a sort of French-Canadian half-breed to whom the Viennese are offering, with trepidation, through the bars of a zoological garden, little mounds of whipped cream.) And *enclaircise* — why, it's as bad as *explicate!* We are right to resent his having made up his own horrors, instead of sticking to the ones that we ourselves employ. But when Whitman says, "I dote on myself, there is that lot of me and all so luscious," we should realize that we are not the only ones who are amused. And the queerly bad and merely queer and queerly good will often change into one another without warning: "Hefts of the moving world, at innocent gambols high and low" — not good, but *queer!* — suddenly becomes, "Something I cannot see puts up libidinous prongs,/ Seas of bright juice suffuse heaven," and it is sunrise.

But it is not in individual lines and phrases, but in passages of some length, that Whitman is at his best. In the following quotation Whitman has something difficult to express, something that there are many formulas, all bad, for expressing; he expresses it with complete success, in language of the most dazzling originality:

The orchestra whirls me wider than Uranus
    flies,
It wrenches such ardors from me I did not
    know I possess'd them,
It sails me, I dab with bare feet, they are
    lick'd by the indolent waves,
I am cut by bitter and angry hail, I lose my
    breath,
Steep'd amid honey'd morphine, my wind-
    pipe throttled in fakes of death,
At length let up again to feel the puzzle of
    puzzles,
And that we call Being.

One hardly knows what to point at — everything works. But *wrenches* and *did not know I possess'd them;* the incredible *it sails me, I dab with bare feet; lick'd by the indolent; steep'd amid honey'd morphine; my windpipe throttled in fakes of death* — no wonder Crane admired Whitman! This originality, as absolute in its way as that of Berlioz'

orchestration, is often at Whitman's command:

I am a dance — play up there! the fit is
    whirling me fast!
I am the ever-laughing — it is new moon and
    twilight,
I see the hiding of douceurs, I see nimble
    ghosts whichever way I look,
Cache and cache again deep in the ground
    and sea, and where it is neither ground
    nor sea.
Well do they do their jobs those journeymen
    divine,
Only from me can they hide nothing, and
    would not if they could,
I reckon I am their boss and they make me
    a pet besides,
And surround me and lead me and run ahead
    when I walk,
To lift their sunning covers to signify me
    with stretch'd arms, and resume the way;
Onward we move, a gay gang of black-
    guards! with mirth-shouting music and
    wild-flapping pennants of joy!

If you did not believe Hopkins' remark about Whitman, that *gay gang of blackguards* ought to shake you. Whitman shares Hopkins' passion for "dappled" effects, but he slides in and out of them with ambiguous swiftness. And he has at his command a language of the calmest and most prosaic reality, one that seems to do no more than present:

The little one sleeps in its cradle.
I lift the gauze and look a long time, and
    silently brush away flies with my hand.
The youngster and the red-faced girl turn
    aside up the bushy hill,
I peeringly view them from the top.

The suicide sprawls on the bloody floor of
    the bed-room.
I witness the corpse with its dabbled hair, I
    note where the pistol has fallen.

It is like magic: that is, something has

been done to us without our knowing how it was done; but if we look at the lines again we see the *gauze, silently, youngster, red-faced, bushy, peeringly, dabbled* — not that this is all we see. "Present! present!" said James; these are presented, put down side by side to form a little "view of life," from the cradle to the last bloody floor of the bedroom. Very often the things presented form nothing but a list:

The pure contralto sings in the organ loft,
The carpenter dresses his plank, the tongue of his foreplane whistles its wild ascending lisp,
The married and unmarried children ride home to their Thanksgiving dinner,
The pilot seizes the king-pin, he heaves down with a strong arm,
The mate stands braced in the whale-boat, lance and harpoon are ready,
The duck-shooter walks by silent and cautious stretches,
The deacons are ordain'd with cross'd hands at the altar,
The spinning-girl retreats and advances to the hum of the big wheel,
The farmer stops by the bars as he walks on a First-day loafe and looks at the oats and rye,
The lunatic is carried at last to the asylum a confirm'd case,
(He will never sleep any more as he did in the cot in his mother's bed-room;)
The jour printer with gray head and gaunt jaws works at his case,
He turns his quid of tobacco while his eyes blur with the manuscript,
The malform'd limbs are tied to the surgeon's table,
What is removed drops horribly in a pail; . . .

It is only a list — but what a list! And how delicately, in what different ways — likeness and opposition and continuation and climax and anticlimax — the transitions are managed, whenever Whitman wants to manage them. Notice them in the next quotation, another "mere list":

The bride unrumples her white dress, the minute-hand of the clock moves slowly,
The opium-eater reclines with rigid head and just-open'd lips,
The prostitute draggles her shawl, her bonnet bobs on her tipsy and pimpled neck. . . .

The first line is joined to the third by *unrumples* and *draggles, white dress* and *shawl;* the second to the third by *rigid head, bobs, tipsy, neck;* the first to the second by *slowly, just-open'd,* and the slowing-down of time in both states. And occasionally one of these lists is metamorphosed into something we have no name for; the man who would call the next quotation a mere list — anybody will feel this — would boil his babies up for soap:

Ever the hard unsunk ground,
Ever the eaters and drinkers, ever the upward and downward sun, ever the air and the ceaseless tides,
Ever myself and my neighbors, refreshing, wicked, real,
Ever the old inexplicable query, ever that thorned thumb, that breath of itches and thirsts,
Ever the vexer's *hoot! hoot!* till we find where the sly one hides and bring him forth,
Ever love, ever the sobbing liquid of life,
Ever the bandage under the chin, ever the trestles of death.

Sometimes Whitman will take what would generally be considered an unpromising subject (in this case, a woman peeping at men in bathing naked) and treat it with such tenderness and subtlety and understanding that we are ashamed of ourselves for having thought it unpromising, and murmur that Chekhov himself couldn't have treated it better:

Twenty-eight young men bathe by the shore,

Twenty-eight young men and all so friendly,
Twenty-eight years of womanly life and all
  so lonesome.

She owns the fine house by the rise of the
  bank,
She hides handsome and richly drest aft the
  blinds of the window.

Which of the young men does she like the
  best?
Ah the homeliest of them is beautiful to her.

Where are you off to, lady? for I see you,
You splash in the water there, yet stay stock
  still in your room.

Dancing and laughing along the beach came
  the twenty-ninth bather,
The rest did not see her, but she saw them
  and loved them.

The beards of the young men glisten'd with
  wet, it ran from their long hair,
Little streams pass'd all over their bodies.

An unseen hand also pass'd over their bodies,
It descended tremblingly from their temples
  and ribs.

The young men float on their backs, their
  white bellies bulge to the sun, they do not
  ask who seizes fast to them,
They do not know who puffs and declines
  with pendant and bending arch,
They do not think whom they souse with
  spray.

And in the same poem (that "Song of
Myself" in which one finds half his best
work) the writer can say of a sea-fight:

Stretch'd and still lies the midnight,
Two great hulls motionless on the breast of
  the darkness,
Our vessel riddled and slowly sinking, preparations to pass to the one we have conquer'd,
The captain on the quarter-deck coldly

giving his orders through a countenance
  white as a sheet,
Near by the corpse of the child that serv'd
  in the cabin,
The dead face of an old salt with long white
  hair and carefully curl'd whiskers,
The flames spite of all that can be done
  flickering aloft and below,
The husky voices of the two or three officers
  yet fit for duty,
Formless stacks of bodies and bodies by
  themselves, dabs of flesh upon the masts
  and spars,
Cut of cordage, dangle of rigging, slight
  shock of the soothe of waves,
Black and impassive guns, litter of powder-
  parcels, strong scent,
A few large stars overhead, silent and mournful shining,
Delicate sniffs of sea-breeze, smells of sedgy
  grass and fields by the shore, death-mes-
  sages given in charge to survivors,
The hiss of the surgeon's knife, the gnawing
  teeth of his saw,
Wheeze, cluck, swash of falling blood, short
  wild scream, and long, dull, tapering
  groan,
These so, these irretrievable.

There are faults in this passage, and they
do not matter: the serious truth, the complete realization of these last lines make
us remember that few poets have shown
more of the tears of things, and the joy
of things, and of the reality beneath
either tears or joy. Even Whitman's most
general or political statements sometimes
are good: everybody knows his "When
liberty goes out of a place it is not the
first to go, nor the second or third to go,/
It waits for all the rest to go, it is the
last"; these sentences about the United
States just before the Civil War may be
less familiar:

Are those really Congressmen? are those the
  great Judges? is that the President?
Then I will sleep awhile yet, for I see that
  these States sleep, for reasons;

(With gathering murk, with muttering thun-
der and lambent shoots we all duly awake,
South, North, East, West, inland and sea-
board, we will surely awake.)

How well, with what firmness and dignity and command, Whitman does such
passages! And Whitman's doubts that he
has done them or anything else well —
ah, there is nothing he does better:

The best I had done seemed to me blank and
suspicious,
My great thoughts as I supposed them, were
they not in reality meagre?
I am he who knew what it was to be evil,
I too knitted the old knot of contrariety . . .
Saw many I loved in the street or ferry-boat
or public assembly, yet never told them a
word,
Lived the same life with the rest, the same
old laughing, gnawing, sleeping,
Played the part that still looks back on the
actor and actress,
The same old role, the role that is what we
make it . . .

Whitman says once that the "look of
the bay mare shames silliness out of me."
This is true — sometimes it is true; but
more often the silliness and affection and
cant and exaggeration are there shame-
lessly, the Old Adam that was in Whitman from the beginning and the awful
new one that he created to keep it company. But as he says, "I know perfectly
well my own egotism,/ Know my omnivorous lines and must not write any less."
He says over and over that there are in
him good and bad, wise and foolish, anything at all and its antonym, and he is
telling the truth; there is in him almost
everything in the world, so that one responds to him, willingly or unwillingly,
almost as one does to the world, that
world which makes the hairs of one's
flesh stand up, which seems both evil

beyond any rejection and wonderful beyond any acceptance. We cannot help
seeing that there is something absurd
about any judgment we make of its
whole — for there is no "point of view"
at which we can stand to make the judgment, and the moral categories that mean
most to us seem no more to apply to its
whole than our spatial or temporal or
causal categories seem to apply to its beginning or its end. (But we need no
arguments to make our judgments seem
absurd — we feel their absurdity without
argument.) In some like sense Whitman
is a world, a waste with, here and there,
systems blazing at random out of the
darkness. Only an innocent and rigidly
methodical mind will reject it for this dis-
organization, particularly since there are
in it, here and there, little systems as
beautifully and astonishingly organized
as the rings and satellites of Saturn:

I understand the large hearts of heroes,
The courage of present times and all times,
How the skipper saw the crowded and rudderless wreck of the steam-ship, and Death
chasing it up and down the storm,
How he knuckled tight and gave not back an
inch, and was faithful of days and faithful of nights,
And chalked in large letters on a board, Be
of good cheer, we will not desert you;
How he follow'd with them and tack'd with
them three days and would not give it up,
How he saved the drifting company at last,
How the lank loose-gown'd women looked
when boated from the side of their prepared graves,
How the silent old-faced infants and the
lifted sick, and the sharp-lipp'd unshaven
men;
All this I swallow, it tastes good, I like it
well, it becomes mine,
I am the man, I suffered, I was there.

In the last lines of this quotation Whitman has reached — as great writers al-

ways reach — a point at which criticism seems not only unnecessary but absurd: these lines are so good that even admiration feels like insolence, and one is ashamed of anything that one can find to say about them. How anyone can dismiss or accept patronizingly the man who wrote them, I do not understand.

The enormous and apparent advantages of form, of omission and selection, of the highest degree of organization, are accompanied by important disadvantages — and there are far greater works than *Leaves of Grass* to make us realize this. But if we compare Whitman with that very beautiful poet Alfred Tennyson, the most skillful of all Whitman's contemporaries, we are at once aware of how limiting Tennyson's forms have been, of how much Tennyson has had to leave out, even in those discursive poems where he is trying to put everything in. Whitman's poems *represent* his world and himself much more satisfactorily than Tennyson's do his. In the past a few poets have both formed and represented, each in the highest degree; but in modern times what controlling, organizing, selecting poet has created a world with as much in it as Whitman's, a world that so plainly *is* the world? Of all modern poets he has, quantitatively speaking, "the most comprehensive soul" — and, qualitatively, a most comprehensive and comprehending one, with charities and concessions and qualifications that are rare in any time.

"Do I contradict myself? Very well then I contradict myself," wrote Whitman, as everybody remembers, and this is not naive, or something he got from Emerson, or a complacent pose. When you organize one of the contradictory elements out of your work of art, you are getting rid not just of it, but of the contradiction of which it was a part; and it is the contradictions in works of art which make them able to represent to us — as logical and methodical generalizations cannot — our world and our selves, which are also full of contradictions. In Whitman we do not get the controlled, compressed, seemingly concordant contradictions of the great lyric poets, of a poem like, say, Hardy's "During Wind and Rain"; Whitman's contradictions are sometimes announced openly, but are more often scattered at random throughout the poems. For instance: Whitman specializes in ways of saying that there is in some sense (a very Hegelian one, generally) no evil — he says a hundred times that evil is not Real; but he also specializes in making lists of the evil of the world, lists of an unarguable reality. After his minister has recounted "the rounded catalogue divine complete," Whitman comes home and puts down what has been left out: "the countless (nineteen-twentieths) low and evil, crude and savage . . . the barren soil, the evil men, the slag and hideous rot." He ends another such catalogue with the plain unexcusing "All these — all meanness and agony without end I sitting look out upon,/ See, hear, and am silent." Whitman offered himself to everybody, and said brilliantly and at length what a good thing he was offering:

Sure as the most certain sure, plumb in the uprights, well entretied, braced in the beams,
Stout as a horse, affectionate, haughty, electrical,
I and this mystery here we stand.

Just for oddness, characteristicalness, differentness, what more could you ask in a letter of recommendation? (Whitman sounds as if he were recommending a house — haunted, but what foundations!) But after a few pages he is oddly different:

Apart from the pulling and hauling stands what I am,
Stands amused, complacent, compassionating, idle, unitary,
Looks down, is erect, or bends an arm on an impalpable certain rest
Looking with side curved head curious what will come next,
Both in and out of the game and watching and wondering at it.

Tamburlaine is already beginning to sound like Hamlet: the employer feels uneasily, "Why, I might as well hire myself. . . ." And, a few pages later, Whitman puts down in ordinary-sized type, in the middle of the page, this warning to any *new person drawn toward me:*

Do you think I am trusty and faithful?
Do you see no further than this façade, this smooth and tolerant manner of me?
Do you suppose yourself advancing on real ground toward a real heroic man?
Have you no thought O dreamer that it may be all maya, illusion?

Having wonderful dreams, telling wonderful lies, was a temptation Whitman could never resist; but telling the truth was a temptation he could never resist, either. When you buy him you know what you are buying. And only an innocent and solemn and systematic mind will condemn him for his contradictions: Whitman's catalogues of evils represent realities, and his denials of their reality represent other realities, of feeling and intuition and desire. If he is faithless to logic, to Reality As It Is — whatever that is — he is faithful to the feel of things, to reality as it seems; this is all that a poet has to be faithful to, and philosophers have been known to leave logic and Reality for it.

Whitman is more coordinate and parallel than anybody, is *the* poet of parallel present participles, of twenty verbs joined by a single subject: all this helps to give his work its feeling of raw hypnotic reality, of being that world which also streams over us joined only by *ands,* until we supply the subordinating conjunctions; and since as children we see the *ands* and not the *becauses,* this method helps to give Whitman some of the freshness of childhood. How inexhaustibly interesting the world is in Whitman! Arnold all his life kept wishing that he could see the world "with a plainness as near, as flashing" as that with which Moses and Rebekah and the Argonauts saw it. He asked with elegiac nostalgia, "Who can see the green earth any more/ As she was by the sources of Time?" — and all the time there was somebody alive who saw it so, as plain and near and flashing, and with a kind of calm, pastoral, Biblical dignity and elegance as well, sometimes. The *thereness* and *suchness* of the world are incarnate in Whitman as they are in few other writers.

They might have put on his tombstone WALT WHITMAN: HE HAD HIS NERVE. He is the rashest, the most inexplicable and unlikely — the most impossible, one wants to say — of poets. He somehow *is* in a class by himself, so that one compares him with other poets about as readily as one compares *Alice* with other books. (Even his free verse has a completely different effect from anybody else's.) Who would think of comparing him with Tennyson or Browning or Arnold or Baudelaire? — it is Homer, or the sagas, or something far away and long ago, that comes to one's mind only to be dismissed; for sometimes Whitman *is* epic, just as *Moby Dick* is, and it surprises us to be able to use truthfully this word that we have misused so many times. Whitman *is* grand, and elevated, and comprehensive, and real with an astonishing reality, and many other things — the critic points at his qualities in despair and wonder, all method failing, and simply calls them by their names. And the range of these qualities is the most extraordinary thing of all. We can surely say about him, "He was a man, take him for all in all. I shall not look upon his like again" — and wish that people had seen this and not tried to be his like: one Whitman is miracle enough, and when he comes again it will be the end of the world.

I have said so little about Whitman's faults because they are so plain: baby critics who have barely learned to complain of the lack of ambiguity in *Peter Rabbit* can tell you all that is wrong with *Leaves of Grass*. But a good many of my readers must have felt that it is ridiculous to write an essay about the obvious fact that Whitman is a great poet. It is ridiculous — just as, in 1851, it would have been ridiculous for anyone to write an essay about the obvious fact that Pope was no "classic of our prose" but a great poet. Critics have to spend half their time reiterating whatever ridiculously obvious things their age or the critics of their age have found it necessary to forget: they say despairingly, at parties, that Wordsworth is a great poet, and *won't* bore you, and tell Mr. Leavis that Milton is a great poet whose deposition *hasn't* been accomplished with astonishing ease by a few words from Eliot. . . . There is something essentially ridiculous about critics, anyway: what is good is good without our saying so, and beneath all our majesty we know this.

Let me finish by mentioning another quality of Whitman's — a quality, delightful to me, that I have said nothing of. If some day a tourist notices, among the ruins of New York City, a copy of *Leaves of Grass*, and stops and picks it up and reads some lines in it, she will be able to say to herself: "How very American! If he and his country had not existed, it would have been impossible to imagine them."

Richard Chase:

WHITMAN AND THE COMIC SPIRIT

In the preface to his Walt Whitman Reconsidered *(1955), Richard Chase explains his emphasis upon "Song of Myself." In the first place, he thinks it is the poet's "greatest and richest work." But he also admits a desire to protest against the "deformed sensibility" of recent years. By this Chase means the taste favorable to works that "display conservative values — the ideal is a well-made poem (or poetic play or novel) full of symbols which admit a religious interpretation." According to this ideal Whitman's elegies are greater poems than "Song of Myself." Chase, on the other hand, prefers writing which "arises out of the native energies and dilemmas of life and is committed to . . . radical literary and cultural values. . . ." Mr. Chase teaches at Columbia University.*

THE main item of the 1855 edition of *Leaves of Grass* was, of course, "Song of Myself," the profound and lovely comic drama of the self which is Whitman's best poem and contains in essence nearly all, yet not quite all, there is to *Leaves of Grass*. The comic spirit of the poem is of the characteristic American sort, providing expression for a realism at once naturalistic and transcendental, for the wit, gaiety, and festive energy of all good comedy, and also for meditative soliloquy, at once intensely personal and strongly generic.

One circumstance that contributes to the general spontaneity of "Song of Myself" is, in fact, Whitman's unsuccessful attempt to be an Emersonian or Wordsworthian moralist. In his preface, he wrote that "of all mankind the poet is the equable man. Not in him but off from him things are grotesque or eccentric or fail of their sanity. . . . He is the arbiter of the diverse and he is the key.

He is the equalizer of his age and land." Whitman tries, indeed, to install himself in his poem on this high moral ground: he will, he says, first regenerate himself by leaving the fallacious artificialities of modern life and getting back to fundamentals; then, having perfected himself as the norm, he will summon all the world to him to be freed of its abnormalities. But although in the poem the self remains pretty much at the center of things, Whitman finds it impossible to accept the idea that it is a norm. To the sententious prophet who "promulges" the normative self, the comic poet and ironic realist keep introducing other, disconcertingly eccentric selves.

Who goes there? hankering, gross, mystical,
    nude. . . .

Whoever he is, he is not in a position to utter morality. The self in this poem *is* (to use Lawrence's phrase) "tricksy-

tricksy"; it does "shy all sorts of ways" and is finally, as the poet says, "not a bit tamed," for "I too am untranslatable." So that as in all true, or high, comedy, the sententious, the too overtly insisted-on morality (if any) plays a losing game with ironical realism. In the social comedy of Moliere, Congreve, or Jane Austen, moral sententiousness, like other deformities of comportment or personality, is corrected by society. But this attitude is, of course, foreign to Whitman, who has already wished to invite society to correct itself by comparing itself with him and who, furthermore, cannot even sustain this democratic inversion of an aristocratic idea. Whitman's comic poetry deflates pretensions and chides moral rigidity by opposing to them a diverse, vital, indeterminate reality.

"I resist anything better than my own diversity," says Whitman, and this is the characteristic note of "Song of Myself." Not that by referring to "Song of Myself" as a "comic" poem I wish too narrowly to limit the scope of discussion — nor do I suggest in using the term a special theory of Whitman or of American literature. I simply respond to my sense that "Song of Myself" is on the whole comic in tone and that although the poem's comic effects are of universal significance, they often take the specific form of American humor. If one finds "Song of Myself" enjoyable at all, it is because one is conscious of how much of the poem, though the feeling in many of its passages need not perhaps have been comic at all, nevertheless appeals to one, first and last, in its comic aspect. The poem is full of odd gestures and whimsical acts; it is written by a neo-Ovidian poet for whom self-metamorphosis is almost as free as free association, who can write "I am an old artillerist" or "I will go to the bank by the wood, and

become undisguised and naked" as easily as he can write:

Askers embody themselves in me and I am
    embodied in them,
I project my hat, sit shame-faced, and beg.

The sense of incongruous diversity is very strong in "Song of Myself," and although one does not know how the sly beggar projecting his hat or the martial patriot is transformed into the "acme of things accomplish'd," and "encloser of things to be" who suddenly says:

I find I incorporate gneiss, coal, long-
    threaded moss, fruits, grains, esculent
    roots,
And am stucco'd with quadrupeds and birds
    all over.

one is nevertheless charmed with the transformation.

Whitman conceives of the self, one might say, as James conceives of Christopher Newman in *The American* — as having the "look of being committed to nothing in particular, of standing in an attitude of general hospitality to the chances of life." In other words, the "self" who is the protagonist of Whitman's poem is a character portrayed in a recognizable American way; it illustrates the fluid, unformed personality exulting alternately in its provisional attempts to define itself and in its sense that it has no definition. The chief difference between "Song of Myself" and *The American* is, of course, the difference between the stages on which Whitman and James allow the self to act, James confining the action to his international scene and Whitman opening his stage out into an eventful universe which is a contradictory but witty collocation of the natural and the transcendent, the imperfect and the utopian, the personal and the generic — a dialectic world out of whose "dimness opposite equals advance" and in which there is "always a knot of identity" but "always distinction."

The very scope of Whitman's universe and the large freedom he assumes to move about in it allowed him to appropriate new areas of experience and thus to make of "Song of Myself" the original and influential poem it is. For one thing, this is the first American poem to invade that fruitful ground between lyric verse and prose fiction that so much of modern poetry cultivates, and one may suppose that "Song of Myself" has had at least as much effect on the novel as, let us say, *Moby Dick* or *The Golden Bowl* have had on poetry. The famous lines in Section 8 are, at any rate, both "imagistic" and novelistic:

The little one sleeps in its cradle; (etc.)

It is probably true that more than anyone else, more than Blake or Baudelaire, Whitman made the city poetically available to literature:

The blab of the pave, tires of carts, sluff of boot-soles, talk of the promenaders,
The heavy omnibus, the driver with his interrogating thumb, the clank of the shod horses on the granite floor . . .

Such lines as these have been multitudinously echoed in modern prose and poetry, they have been endlessly recapitulated by the journey of the realistic movie camera up the city street. One might argue that Whitman's descriptions of the city made possible T. S. Eliot's *Waste Land*. The horror of Eliot's London, as of Baudelaire's "*cité pleine de rêves*," is unknown in *Leaves of Grass*, but was not Whitman the first poet, so

to speak, who put real typists and clerks in the imaginery city?

There can be no doubt that "Song of Myself" made sex a possible subject for American literature, and in this respect Whitman wrought a great revolution in, for example, his beautiful idyllic scene in which the "handsome and richly drest" woman imagines herself to join the "twenty-eight young men" who "bathe by the shore." In such a passage as this (as Henry Adams was to point out) American literature was moving toward the freedom and inclusiveness that came more naturally to Europeans — to Flaubert, or Chekhov, whose panoramic novelette *The Steppe* includes a similarly idyllic scene of bathing and sexuality. It is sex, too, although of an inverted kind, that allows Whitman to write the following unsurpassable lines in which love is at once so sublimely generalized and perfectly particularized:

And [I know] that a kelson of the creation is love,
And limitless are leaves stiff or drooping in the fields,
And brown ants in the little wells beneath them,
And mossy scabs of the worm fence, and heap'd stones, elder, mullein and pokeweed.

No summary view of "Song of Myself" would be complete without reference to the elegiac tone of the concluding lines. If, as we have been saying, Whitman's poem is remarkable for its gross inclusive scope, his elegiac verse is a great act of discrimination and nicety. Where else, in the generally grandiose nineteenth-century melodrama of love and death shall we find anything like the delicate precision of these incomparable lines?

The last scud of day holds back for me;

It flings my likeness after the rest and true
as any, on the shadow'd wilds, (etc.)

As every poet does, Whitman asks us
provisionally to accept the imagined
world of his poem. It is a fantastic world
in which it is presumed that the self can
become identical with all other selves
in the universe, regardless of time and
space. Not without precedent in Hindu
poetry, this central metaphor is, as an
artistic device, unique in American literature, as is the extraordinary collection
of small imagist poems, versified short
stories, realistic urban and rural genre
paintings, inventories, homilies, philoso-
phizings, farcical episodes, confessions,
and lyric musings it encompasses in
"Song of Myself." Yet as heavily taxing
our powers of provisional credence, as
inventing a highly idiosyncratic and illusory world, "Song of Myself" invites comparison with other curious works of the
American imagination — *Moby Dick,* let
us say, and *The Scarlet Letter* and *The
Wings of the Dove.* It is of the first
importance at any rate to see that Whitman's relation of the self to the rest of
the universe is a successful aesthetic or
compositional device, whatever we may
think of it as a moral assertion.

If we look at Whitman's implicit metaphor more closely, we see that it consists
in the paradox of "identity." The opening
words of *Leaves of Grass,* placed there
in 1867, state the paradox:

One's-self I sing, a simple separate person,
Yet utter the word Democratic, the word
En-Masse.

In more general terms the opening lines
of "Song of Myself" state the same
paradox:

I celebrate myself and sing myself;
And what I assume you shall assume;

For every atom belonging to me, as good
belongs to you.

Both politically and by nature man has
"identity," in two senses of the word:
on the one hand, he is integral in himself,
unique, and separate; on the other hand,
he is equal to, or even the same as, everyone else. Like the Concord transcendentalists, Whitman was easily led in
prophetic moods to generalize the second
term of the paradox of identity beyond
the merely human world and with his
ruthless equalitarianism to conceive the
All, a vast cosmic democracy, placid,
without episode, separation or conflict,
though suffused, perhaps, with a bland
illumination. More than anything else,
it is this latter tendency which finally
ruined Whitman as a poet, submerging
as it did, his chief forte and glory — his
entirely original, vividly realistic presentation of the comedy and pathos of "the
simple separate person."

What finally happens is that Whitman
loses his sense that his metaphor of
self vs. en-masse is a *paradox,* that self
and en-masse are in dialectic opposition.
When this sense is lost the spontaneously
eventful, flowing, and largely indeterminate universe of "Song of Myself" is
replaced by a universe that is both
mechanical and vaguely abstract. Whatever, in this universe, is in a state of
becoming is moving toward the All, and
the self becomes merely the vehicle by
which the journey is made.

In some of his best as well as in some
of his worst poems, Whitman actually
conceives of the self as making a journey
— for example, "Song of the Open Road,"
"Crossing Brooklyn Ferry," and "Passage
to India." In others the self journeys, as
it were, not forward and outward but
backward and inward, back to the roots
of its being, and discovers there a final

mystery, or love, comradeship, or death — for example, the *Calamus* and *Sea Drift* poems. (Notably among the latter are "Out of the Cradle Endlessly Rocking" and "As I Ebb'd with the Ocean of Life.") In "Song of Myself," however, the self is not felt to be incomplete; it has no questing odyssey to make. It stands aggressively at the center of things, "Sure as the most certain sure, plumb in the uprights, well entretied, braced in the beams." It summons the universe, "syphons" universal experience through its dilating pores, calls "anything back again when I desire it." Or the self imagines itself to be infinitely expandable and contractible (like the web of the spider in Whitman's little poem called "A Noiseless Patient Spider"), so that there is no place where at any moment it may not be, no thing or person with whom it may not merge, no act in which it may not participate. Of great importance is the fact that most of "Song of Myself" has to do not with the self searching for a final identity but with the self escaping a series of identities which threaten to destroy its lively and various spontaneity. This combination of attitudes is what gives "Song of Myself" the alternately ecstatic and gravely musing, pastoral-godlike stability one feels at the center, around which, however, the poet is able to weave the most astonishing embellishments of wit and lyric song.

This is perhaps a valid way of feeling the shifting modes of sensibility in the poem. Yet it would be wrong to attribute any clear cut structure to "Song of Myself." "The United States themselves are essentially the greatest poem," wrote Whitman in his preface. A Jacksonian Democrat, Whitman was not an admirer of federal unity, either in a nation or a poem. He was content to make his poem a loose congeries of states and half-settled territories. He was content that his poem should mirror that "freshness and candor of . . . physiognomy," that "picturesque looseness of carriage," and that "deathless attachment to freedom" which, in his preface, he attributed to his countrymen. His style would be organic; he would "speak in literature with the perfect rectitude and insouciance" of animals and growing things. Although capable of finely pictorial images, Whitman composed more by ear than by eye, and his ear being attuned to music of the looser, more variable sort, such as the Italian operas, he strung his poems together on a free melodic line and by means of motifs, voices, recapitulations, recitatives, rests, *crescendi* and *diminuendi*.

The motif of "Song of Myself" is the self taking on a bewildering variety of identities and with a truly virtuoso agility extricating itself from each one. The poem begins with the exhortation to leave the "rooms full of perfume," the "creeds and schools." Apart from conventions,

Apart from the pulling and hauling stands what I am,
Stands amused, complacent, compassionating, idle, unitary.

Having put society and convention behind, "What I am" finds itself in an Edenlike, early-morning world, wherein one easily observes the portentous dialectics of the universe:

Urge and urge and urge,
Always the procreant urge of the world.
Out of the dimness opposite equals advance, always substance and increase, always sex,
Always a knit of identity, always distinction, always a breed of life.

But of more importance is the fact that in this idyllic world the veil is lifted from the jaundiced eye, the cramped sensibility is set free, the senses and pores of the body receive the joyful intelligences dispatched to them by a friendly and providential nature. The self appears to be the offspring of a happy union of body and soul; sublime and delightful thoughts issue from the mind in the same miraculous way as the grass from the ground. Death itself is seen to be "lucky." And, in short, "what I am" can well afford to be complacent, to be certain that it is "unitary." Nor is the feeling of power denied to the self. It derives power from nature, as does the horse — "affectionate, haughty, electrical" — with which the poet compares himself. It derives power, too, from identification with others — the "runaway slave," "the butcher-boy," the "blacksmiths," "the boatmen and clam-diggers," the "trapper," the "red girl" — and finally with America itself.

In me the caresser of life wherever moving,
  backward as well as forward sluing,
To niches aside and junior bending, not a
  person or object missing,
Absorbing all to myself and for this song.

Sections 24–28, though in places rather obscure, contain the essence of Whitman's drama of identity. The poet begins by proclaiming himself a Kosmos, and commanding us to "unscrew the locks from the doors! Unscrew the doors themselves from their jambs!" so that the universe may flow through him — "through me the current and index" (that is, the undifferentiated flux and the "identities" that emerge therefrom). This proclamation announces not only the unshakable status and palpable reality but also the redemptive powers of the self. In a world which has been created by banishing social sanctions and social intelligence, what will keep man from being lost in idiocy, crime, squalor? What of that underground realm inhabited by

. . . the deform'd, trivial, flat, foolish, despised,
Fog in the air, beetles rolling balls of dung?

The threat of madness, crime, and obscenity is to be allayed by the curative powers of that Adamic world where wisdom consists in uttering "the password primeval," "the sign of democracy." Siphoned through the haughty, electrical self or discussed frankly by persons not inhibited by prudery (the discourses seem perilously interchangeable), the crimes and obscenities will be redeemed:

Voices indecent by me clarified and transfigur'd.

The poet then records a dreamlike idyl of auto-erotic experience, in which the parts of the body merge mysteriously with natural objects, and a great deal of diffuse and wistful love is generated. And, when dawn comes, the redemption is symbolized in these astonishing metaphors:

Hefts of the moving world at innocent gambols silently rising, freshly exuding,
Scooting obliquely high and low.
Something I cannot see puts upward libidinous prongs,
Seas of bright juice suffuse heaven.

The poem then speaks anew of how the self may be distorted or destroyed. The poet's "identity" is said to be assailed and warped into other "identities" by agents referred to as "traitors," "wasters," and "marauders." Somewhat elusive in particular, these appear to have in common a quality of aggressiveness and imperiousness. They act as a radical individu-

alist conceives society to act. They break
down the self, they swagger, they assert
convention, responsibility and reason,
they dominate and impose passivity and
furtiveness on the individual.

The beautiful, diffuse, kindly dawn is
succeeded by a more formidable, a more
imperious, apparition. The "dazzling and
tremendous" sun leaps over the horizon
and cries, "See then whether you shall
be master!" The poet replies to this
challenge by saying that the sunrise
would indeed "kill me / If I could not
now and always send sunrise out of me."
The power with which the poet defeats
what seeks to destroy him is asserted to
be "my vision" and "my voice."

My voice goes after what my eyes cannot
    reach,
With the twirl of my tongue I encompass
    worlds.

In Section 26 both the metaphorical
effects and the subject matter shift from
the visual to the auditory. The "bravuras
of birds, bustle of growing wheat, gossip
of flames, clack of sticks cooking my
meals" — these and myriad other sounds
amplify into a symphonic orchestration.
The crescendo and dying fall of the
conclusion are rendered with full tone
and exquisite wit.

I hear the train'd soprano (what work, with
    hers, is this?)
The orchestra whirls me wider than Uranus
    flies,
It wrenches such ardors from me I did not
    know I possess'd them,
It sails me, I dab with bare feet, they are
    lick'd by the indolent waves,
I am cut by bitter and angry hail, I lose my
    breath,
Steep'd amid honey'd morphine, my wind-
    pipe throttled in fakes of death,
At length let up again to feel the puzzle of
    puzzles,

And that we call Being.

But again the poet is confronted with
"Being" — that is, form or identity — and
is not certain that this is the Being he
wants to be. It is therefore dissipated
and generalized, in Section 27, into a
universal process of reincarnation.

In Section 28 there occurs the famous
auto-erotic pastoral dream in which "prurient provokers," like nibbling cows,
"graze at the edges of me." The "provokers," conceived as symbolic of the
sense of touch, arouse and madden the
dreaming poet and then they all unite
"to stand on a headland and worry me."
After touch has "quivered" him "to a new
identity" — has left him confused, vexed,
self-reproachful, and isolated — he proceeds in the following sections to resume
a "true," "real," or "divine" identity. This
act of restoration is accomplished
through love, natural piety, pastoral and
cosmic meditations, symbolic fusions of
self with America, allegations of the "deific" nature of democratic man, ritual
celebrations, and fatherly preachments,
and finally, in the last Section, by the
assertion that death is also merely an
extrication of the self from an identity.

Everyone has noticed that the large,
bland exterior of Walt Whitman concealed a Dionysus or Pan — one of the
first was Moncure Conway, who visited
Walt in Brooklyn in the summer of 1857,
found him basking in the sun on a hill
near the Whitman house, and later
noticed that the only decorations in the
poet's room were two engravings, "one
of Silenus and the other of Bacchus."
And surely no one can read "Song of
Myself" without seeing that Whitman
recreates there something of the spirit of
the Greek cults out of which comedy
evolved. Does he not summon us, his
boon companions, to the outdoor revel,

to "dance, laugh, and sing," to celebrate the phallic god? Are not masks donned and removed, "identities" concealed and exchanged? Do we not have a ritual celebration of "Nature without check with original energy," of the cycle of death and rebirth, the *agon,* sacrifice, and *gamos* of the protagonist, i.e. the self? Do we not have in Whitman's image of the diffusion of the self in nature a religious feeling akin to that engendered in the Dionysian mysteries by the dismemberment and assimilation of the sacrificial victim?

To be sure, the "mysticism" we ordinarily associate with Whitman is less akin to Dionysian than to Oriental and Quaker religion. His mode of religious contemplation, taking it by and large, tends toward passivity and quietism. There is much of this quietism even in "Song of Myself." But the poem as a whole takes its tone from something more vital, indeterminate, violent, and primitive. And it is only to find the most appropriate name for this that one hits on the word "Dionysian." The ritual submovement of comedy asserts itself with a brilliant if spasmodic energy in "Song of Myself." It provides a metaphorical foundation for even the most elaborately artificial of verbal fancies such as "I recline by the sills of the exquisite flexible doors" or "I depart as air. I shake my white locks at the runaway sun" — lines which in point of rococo refinement rival anything that Congreve's Millamant might say to Mirabell.

Historically, Whitman's "American humor" is indeed related, however remotely, to the Restoration comedy. Broadly speaking, there have been in English since 1660 three manifestations of the comic spirit: the aristocratic high comedy of Congreve, the bourgeois sentimental or genteel comedy (by far the most pervasive and influential sort ever since the Restoration), and that American humor which has been practiced in one way or another and at one time or another by nearly all of our best writers. This is not the place to attempt a history of comedy or an analysis of American humor — the latter has been done exquisitely, if a little impressionistically, by Constance Rourke. One may merely venture the idea that, historically, American humor is a radical modification of sentimental comedy. At its best — in Mark Twain, Melville, Thoreau, or Whitman — it retains the capacity of sentimental comedy for pathos but escapes its sentimentality and its hypocrisy. It achieved this by rejecting the cardinal ethical values of bourgeois comedy — money and domestic fidelity. American humor is contemptuous of, or at least feels remote from, the family and money as ethical norms. In this respect and in its tendency toward cruelty and sheer verbal brilliance it is akin to high comedy.

Considered as a comic poem, "Song of Myself" combines Dionysian gaiety and an impulse toward verbal artificiality with the tone and cultural presuppositions of American humor — a striking feat of hybridization certainly, yet no more so than that which produced *Moby Dick.* The intention here is not to deny the justice of Emerson's remark that Whitman's poem was "a remarkable mixture of the *Bhagvatgeeta* and the *New York Herald*" or of the voluminous but one-sided academic scholarship which, following Emerson's remark, has regarded "Song of Myself" as an amalgam of Oriental philosophy and American realism. The intention is rather to shift the ground of discourse toward a more strictly literary view — the view which Emerson also adumbrated in his remark that the first edition of *Leaves of Grass* was an "extraordinary piece of wit and wisdom."

In 1889 Whitman said to his Camden friends, "I pride myself on being a real humorist underneath everything else" and when it was suggested that he might after all go down in history as a "come-dian" he replied that one "might easily end up worse." He will certainly not go down in history as, purely and simply, a comedian. But humor was always a strong part of his sensibility, and it is difficult to see how it ever came to be a cliché about Whitman that "he had no sense of humor." There is substantial evidence that in his early life his mind turned naturally toward comic writing. Much of his newspaper work, particu-larly the "Sun-Down Papers From the Desk of a Schoolmaster," which he wrote for the *Long Island Democrat* and the sketches he did for the New Orleans *Crescent* (1848) show that he had mas-tered at least the easier tricks of the native folk humor. At various times dur-ing the 1840's Whitman expressed in newspaper articles his partiality to Dick-ens and Carlyle — Dickens whom "I love and esteem . . . for what he has taught me through his writings"; Carlyle, whose *Sartor Resartus* exhibits in abundance the author's "strange wild way." From these two writers Whitman seems to have learned that a great book might be elo-quent, crotchety, full of curious events and observations, or a humorous com-pound of realism, philosophy, and senti-ment. He surely learned this even more directly from Emerson's essays. If indeed there are so many parallels between "Song of Myself" and "Self-Reliance" that we almost think the poem a versification of the essay, it is nevertheless true that the parallels are not confined to the philosophic or moral message. There is a good deal of humor in Emerson's essay

of the spontaneous, odd, yeasty sort noticed by Santayana, who said that Emerson "was like a young god making experiments in creation: he botched the work and always began on a new and better plan. Every day he said, 'Let there be light,' and every day the light was new." More specifically, what Whitman may have sensed in "Self-Reliance" is the humorous touch-and-go between the self and the author, which underlies the elab-orate web of portentous epigram. Surely, one of the Emersonian passages that brought the simmering Whitman to a boil (as the poet himself phrased it) was the one near the end of "Self-Reliance" where Emerson is speaking of the fatuity of foreign travel and says that although he should wake up in Naples, "there beside me is the stern fact, the sad self, unrelenting, identical, that I fled from."

But aside from the question of literary influences there is the more fundamental question of cultural influence. Whitman emulated our democratic American ideals to an extent unexampled among our great writers, and there can be no doubt that many of his moral utterances and even his poetic effects are produced by the sublime literalness of the democratic assumptions which were so faithfully registered on his plastic mind and tem-perament. Tocqueville . . . based a part of his discussion of language and litera-ture in the United States upon his obser-vation that

In democratic communities each citizen is habitually engaged in the contemplation of a very puny object, namely, himself. If he ever raises his looks higher, he then per-ceives nothing but the immense form of society at large, or the still more imposing aspect of mankind. His ideas are all either extremely minute and clear, or extremely general and vague; what lies between is an open void.

This habit of mind has induced in American writing a style capable of very great and sudden extremes and has drawn from such writers as Melville, Emerson, Thoreau, and Emily Dickinson their idiosyncratic styles — the common denominator among them being a tendency of the language to shift rapidly from the homely and the colloquial to a rhetoric at once highly self-conscious, highly abstract, and highly elaborate. Since such shifts of ground between incongruous extremes are of the essence of wit, it is proper to speak of wit, or as we say, of "American humor," as a central problem in any exact investigation of the language of American literature — so long as we keep in mind how very pervasive an attitude is American humor. For indeed this form of wit is not confined to rural hoe-downs, minstrel shows, or tall tales about Paul Bunyan. It is a style, a habit of thought which allows for the different combinations of the native vernacular and traditional English created by the American authors, as well as their common habit of shifting with such brilliant effect from the particular to the general, from the small to the great, from the concrete to the transcendent. To encompass such effects a language must be highly flexible, capable not of subtle and sustained modulations, as is the prose of Edmund Burke or the poetry of Shakespeare,* but — as Selincourt observed in writing about Whitman's language — of rapid transpositions, rapid shifts of language and of levels of discourse. And if these remarks are generally true of all American authors, they seem more literally true of Whitman than of anyone else.

* Shakespeare's style, wrote Whitman (sounding for the moment like Burke) is determined by "the exquisite and seductive transfiguration of caste."

Thus Whitman's struggle for a language in the years before 1855 was not essentially different from that of his peers among American writers. It was easy to combine the literary with the vernacular as a joke, and Whitman often did this in his newspaper writing, as in (a sentence from one of his New Orleans sketches) "a beautiful, enameled, filigree, inlaid morceau of *bijouterie,* whose value intrinsically, per se, was perhaps about six bits," or "we will e'en just have to give the go-by." It was more difficult to learn the trick of producing similar transpositions without being silly or bethetic — such a trick as is turned toward the end of "Song of Myself" where the last line of Section 43 and the first of 44 are:

Nor the present, nor the least wisp that is known.
It is time to explain myself — let us stand up.

And most difficult of all was to achieve the standard accomplishment of the poetry at its best — a style, that is, which is "literary" and conversational at the same time, a style which has one eye on the individual and the concrete and one eye on the general and the transcendent.

One had better hasten to admit that a good deal of caution is called for in arguments which adduce the culture a poet lives in to explain his aesthetics. For one thing, it is of course impossible to say just what American culture is or to be sure that one traces aright its manifold influences on poetry. Then, again, no culture is perfectly unique. France has had democratic poets, there are moments in Rabelais and Kafka which seem indistinguishable from "American humor," Heine and Arnold wrote relatively "free verse," Whitman's own ideals were not only national but international. Yet the fact remains that we do have an observable national culture as well as an inherited European one, and that a truly historical critique of Whitman's poetry must begin with a view of the spoken and unspoken assumptions, the myths and habits of mind, the manners and "sentiments," of the culture the poet lived in.

Even Whitman's notion of the poet as the passive recipient of inspiration who merely utters without conscious artifice the song which possesses him is to be understood as peculiarly compatible with a democratic society. For the democrat automatically assumes himself to be the fully accredited representative and spokesman of his country, and thus he is easily disposed to believe, when he becomes a poet, that his country, mankind, and the universe itself speak through him. This is the assumption of Whitman's Preface, where we read that "The greatest poet has less a marked style, and is more the channel of thoughts and things without increase or diminution." One of the paradoxes of American democracy is that though it is the product of a high civilization it is conducive to an idea of the poet which belongs rather to the age of the muses than to later periods. This is one of our ways of returning to the primitive sources of the imagination, and it operated in Whitman along with two other tendencies in the same direction — the "inner light" of the Quakers and the romantic or transcendental theory of poetic "possession."

In what sense is Whitman a mythic poet? "Great are the myths" of the past, he wrote in a poem originally included in the 1855 edition. But, he adds, great also are the myths of democracy, and the democratic poet must assert not only the myths of "the risen and fallen nations" but also Liberty, Equality, Day and Night, Truth, Language, Law, Justice, Life, and, of "the greatest purport,"

Death. The reader of this poem will surely reflect that if Adam and Eve, Dionysus and Zeus are the creatures of myth, we appear to be confronted with something else when Liberty and Equality (not personifications but pure abstractions) are substituted for these personages. An indispensable characteristic of myth is its air of having a past, of retaining the aura of a primitive time which either has or is imagined to have historically existed. A poem about Zeus is of no interest if it fails to recapture a sense of the primitive religious feeling. And Whitman's culture had, properly speaking, no primitive age.

Still, we are correct in thinking, as did the poet himself, that there are mythic elements in "Song of Myself," as throughout Leaves of Grass (although it might be well, but for the awkwardness of the phrase, to refer to Whitman's "pseudo-myths"). There is no population of glamorous or semidivine persons; but there are emergent generic persons of the kind discerned by Edward Dowden, one of Whitman's first foreign admirers, when he wrote that "the mettlesome, proud, turbulent, brash, self-asserting young Achilles, lover of women and lover of comrades, of Whitman's epic, can be no other than the American people; the Ulysses, the prudent, the 'cute, the battler with the forces of nature, the traveller in the sea-like prairie, desolate swamp and dense forest is brother Jonathan." And, as Dowden might have added, there is the self, a dramatic presence called Walt Whitman, "hankering, gross, mystical, nude."

And if "Song of Myself" invokes a future instead of a past, it nevertheless adduces a kind of generalized primitive age as it goes along. Whitman does this partly in the usual, or Virgilian, manner — he adduces legends, that is, from the national past as in the passages about the Alamo and Bunker Hill. But far more striking and pervasive is his poetically bold assertion of a flowing universe in which the primitive and the civilized seem to be interchangeable or contemporaneous. This entails, of course, an inevitable artificiality and it encourages an elaborate fancifulness — which is why the mythic elements in Whitman's poems, as in many more modern works, impress one as being contrived *ad hoc.* In a country like ancient Greece, where history reached back into a native barbarism, the most sophisticated literature could be made to reverberate a copious mythology. But the American writer, who, like Cooper, Melville, Mark Twain, Hawthorne, Parkman, Faulkner, or Hemingway, includes in his temperament the myth-making tendency, has to rely on the few modes of genuine myth-producing experience America offers — such as, the Odyssey-like whale or bear hunt or flight down the river, the frontier legends, or the deeply imbedded customs of the old South or early New England — and contrive the rest as his genius will allow. Although actually he was much more citified than any of his peers among the great American authors, Whitman shared with them Thoreau's ideas on "wildness."

Walking "west," in his sublimely imaginary manner, Thoreau reflected that "In literature it is only the wild that attracts us. Dullness is but another name for tameness. It is the uncivilized free and wild thinking in 'Hamlet' and the 'Iliad,' in all the Scriptures and Mythologies, not learned in the schools, that delights us." Whitman's poems show the tendency toward the mythic and emblematic which has transformed in American hands so many potential "novels" into "romances" and so many poems into prophecies. Yet Whitman makes much

less consistent use of the available mythic motifs than he might (although the camerado on the open road might be considered a version of the Odyssey motif).

Generally speaking, Whitman's method is to mythicize the abstractions of democratic idealism. For Whitman, equality, freedom, and fraternity are pervasive and magical laws vibrantly revealed in the visible universe; and the self is a preternatural being, a numenous presence which is felt with all the wonder the primitive man feels in the presence of his god or tutelary spirit.

In the sense, then, that it mythicizes, not primitive intuitions and fundamental human dilemmas, but abstract ideas which are the product of ages of civilization, "Song of Myself" is the most contrived and artificial of American mythic fictions. There is no dramatic sense of the past, no pathos of a past being destroyed before one's eyes, as there is in the work of other American mythicists. There is no real temporal dimension in the poem. Even "the future" is more honorific, something praised and insisted on, than temporal. There is instead a kind of timeless emergence, which allows the poet to make the logically and historically preposterous but poetically valid assertion that past and present exist contemporaneously. By a vast *tour de force* Whitman makes us believe that American democracy, the product of Christianity and European enlightenment, exists in a half-urban, half-pastoral world of primeval novelty, where the blessed and unfallen inhabitants gather to hear the songs and preachments of the bard, as the people of the forest gathered about Orpheus. For this poet, the products of a high civilization — science, skepticism, evolution, the belief in equality and progress — are convertible into the images of a primeval mythic vision. (Intellectually, it must be admitted, this attitude is no different from that of countless provincial and unlettered people of our New World — those restless, aspiring, crankish persons who confuse science with magic, atheism with religion, biases and crotchets with thought, who read, as Whitman did, Voltaire, Franklin, Tom Paine, and Robert Ingersoll, who take up pseudo-sciences like phrenology, as Whitman did, and who, like Whitman in his late years, tend to confine their discussion of Shakespeare to the "Baconian controversy." Fortunately the transfiguring powers of poetry are inexhaustible.)

The national literature — witness Poe, Melville, Emerson, James — has been distinguished by its concern with the self. Our optimistic moralists and philosophers have thought of the redeemed, healthy, spontaneous self as the nearly sufficient assurance of an ever improving and one-day ideal social order. Our poets and novelists have posed the question of selfhood and made ghosts and symbols out of the self, the other self, the *doppelgänger,* the ideal self, the evil self in a great variety of ways. Yet it was left to Whitman to make of the self the new mythic principle which is one of his chief claims of originality.

As a moralist Whitman shares with Emerson his belief that the self can be self-sufficient and that merely by being good, free, various, spontaneous, and loving enough, it can extrude, as it were, the good society. Speaking of the effect upon the conception of the self entailed in the transcendentalists' view of nature, society, and the individual, Mr. Quentin Anderson has written: "Under the pressure engendered by packing nature, history, providence, creativity, and political and moral sanctions into it, the self . . . becomes a species of universal register

or 'transparent eyeball' [the phrase is Emerson's], and the capacity for a dramatic, an actively social life, seems to disappear altogether." Mr. Anderson, who would doubtless extend his view to include Whitman, is right to object to what is morally speaking so hazardous an overestimation of what the unaccommodated self can accomplish.

But in "Song of Myself" Whitman's moral dubiety is his poetic plenitude. The transcendentalist trick of making the self "a species of universal register" is Whitman's triumph in "Song of Myself." Whitman's fanciful idea that the self is able to assume the imprint of any "identity" it wishes without regard to the barriers of space or time and thus to provide for the transformation of the simple separate person into the democratic en-masse or community of comrades was, as a conceit or mythic conception, a stunning novelty. It allowed him to reconstitute the mythic imagination on new ground. T. S. Eliot apparently regards Whitman's claim to originality, at least of poetic language, as spurious. But it must be noted that *The Waste Land* is not the first "universal" English poem loosely organized by a stream-of-consciousness or musical technique, having a protagonist called "I" who merges regardless of time and space with a variety of historic and mythical personages, and celebrating the recurring cycles of death and rebirth — "Song of Myself" is. This thematic similarity need not be pressed as a case of Whitman's "influence"; two poems could hardly be more dissimilar in tone. The affinity seems rather to be a coincidence of two very different minds asking the same implicit question: What, in a spiritually eclectic, already Alexandrian, "American" world, is the status and fate of the self? It is probable, one may add, that both

"Song of Myself" and *The Waste Land* were influenced by the *Bhagavad Gita,* which may be loosely described as thematically similar to these two poems.

A more direct influence of Whitman is that upon Joyce. *Finnegans Wake,* the culminating work, the summa of the contemporary mythic movement in literature (and in some ways, it must be admitted, its *reductio ad absurdum*) seems confessedly to owe a debt to Whitman. The bard referred to as "old Whiteman self" (p. 263) is made to say (p. 551) "I foredreamed for thee and more than fullmaked: I prevented for thee in the haunts that joybelled grail light-a-leaves. . . ." And indeed the "panromain* apological which Watllwewhistlem sang" may easily have suggested to Joyce how a work of literature might picture "the soul of everyelsesbody rolled into its olesoleself." Humphrey Chimpden Earwicker, Joyce's protagonist, has the same capacity as the "I" of "Song of Myself" to merge ("at no spatial time") with and become anyone and anything in the universe. The drawer of parallels might well begin with Sections 27–31 of "Song of Myself," where, for example, he will find Whitman referring to reincarnation thus:

To be in any form, what is that?
(Round and round we go, all of us, and ever come back thither.)

— an interesting analogue of Joyce's "The Vico road goes round an round to meet where terms begin." In a very real sense, then, *Finnegans Wake* is the ultimate development of a literary method "foredreamed" in "Song of Myself." This fact serves to remind us that various and

* Presumably — pan-Roman (i.e., "universal") and pan-romaine (i.e., a vegetable: "Leaves of Grass") and pan-*roman* (the universal novel).

valuable as the mythic movement in literature has been, it seems finally to run into the sands and to be cherished only by a small number of readers. It is ironic in view of Whitman's desire for a universal audience that he should have furnished what is from one point of view the first example of so special a kind of literature. But it is historically significant that the affinity between Whitman and Joyce should be an affinity of comic sensibility. The references to Whitman in *Finnegans Wake* (brief as they are) are fresher and more moving to the modern reader than are those, for example, in Hart Crane's *The Bridge,* where Whitman is understood only as the aspirational prophet.

Whitman was, of course, nothing like the modern poets in point of conscious technical sophistication. His practice was sometimes highly sophisticated, but his theory was either fragmentary and hesitating or nonexistent. One poetic device which did interest him and which he reflected on at length (doubtless with the encouragement of Emerson's essays on Nature and the Poet) was the use of words "indirectly" — that is, as "hieroglyphics," "symbols," or implied myths. Whitman conceived of language as he conceived of the universe. It was a flow — "that huge English flow," as he called it in the open letter to Emerson which he appended to the 1856 edition of *Leaves of Grass.* Words are "magical" or "spiritual" when they first emerge, as "identities," from the flow. All words, as he had learned from Emerson, were originally poetic metaphors. And it is the business of the bard to speak words from which the sensuous poetic and "spiritual" quality has not been lost or to revivify words from which it has. This "real first-class poet," said Whitman, reviewing his own book in 1855, has hit upon a new scheme which is more "subtle" than the presentation of "acts and events" by Homer or of "characters" by Shakespeare. "Every sentence and every passage" of this poet "tells of an interior not always seen, and exudes an impalpable something which sticks to him that reads, and pervades and provokes him to tread the half-invisible road where the poet, like an apparition, is striding fearlessly before." This transcendentalist or prophetic illusion is to be created by using words still redolent of the essence of that universal flow of unconscious thought from which all words emerge. Words, poetic thoughts, thus originate as miraculously as do the leaves of grass. Indeed, the objects of nature, particularly phallic objects, are called, in "Spontaneous Me" (1856), "real poems." Like all natural things, "all words are spiritual . . ." he wrote in *An American Primer*. And like natural things they have a history, an evolution. "Whence are they? along how many thousand and tens of thousands of years have they come? those eluding, fluid, beautiful, fleshless, realities, Mother, Father, Water, Earth, Me, This, Soul, Tongue, House, Fire."

In Whitman's view of language (which is clear, it must be admitted, only in its general outlines), colloquial words best unite the "natural" and the "spiritual." Therefore the poet will use words in such a way as to give them the freshness, raciness, and mythic significance of colloquial speech. Such seems to be Whitman's argument in his "Slang of America," an essay of especial interest in relation to "Song of Myself." Slang he understands to be "the lawless germinal element below all words and sentences, and behind all poetry," which provides "a certain perennial rankness and protestantism in speech." What he heard among the common people he took to be

the genesis of poetry: "the wit — the rich flashes of humor and genius." The poet will use language as the earliest people did when colloquial words — the "living and buried speech," as he says in "Song of Myself" — were incipient myths, when they "gave the start to, and perfected, the whole immense tangle of the old mythologies." Characteristically Whitman thought of these incipient myths as having a comic element.

Thus in his ideas about words, as in his poetic practice, Whitman is paradoxically extremely civilized and extremely primitive. Both semanticist and bard, he is a kind of primitive I. A. Richards and a sophisticated Orpheus. As a poet who wishes to create a mythic poetry he is confronted with the dilemma (the democratic dilemma, Tocqueville would say) of a sensibility which quickens to mythic feeling only at opposite ends of the spectrum, either in spontaneous, inchoate, "germinal" experience or in abstractions such as Mother, Father, Equality, Love or Democracy. What he lacks, as compared with Homer, for example, or Dante or Milton, is a mediating body of mythic narrative and metaphor. All such mediating metaphors struck Whitman as "feudal" and therefore improper in democratic poetry. It was what he took to be the positive advantage of this attitude that led him to describe his poems as more "subtle" than Homer with his poetry of "acts and events" and Shakespeare with his poetry of "characters."

Having given up so much — so much more, indeed, than his democratic situation forced him to give up — Whitman is reduced to two principal stratagems of mediation — his use of words in a mythic-semantic manner, as if he were Adam naming the animals, and his one grand narrative and metaphorical image of the self with its dialectic powers and its eternal vitality and significance. Not, of course, that these stratagems are his whole stock in trade; rather, he sets them triumphantly in opposition to the traditional techniques which remain in his poetry and which he always found necessary but which, nevertheless, he could never succeed with when he used them alone. When Whitman writes badly it is either because he is trying to get along without his own stratagems (as in "O Captain, my Captain") or because he is misusing them. Anyone who asks sheer words to do so much cannot help debasing the currency and sometimes producing mere lifeless lists of names. As Matthiessen pointed out, he also runs the risk of writing nonsense — for instance, such a line as

O for you whoever you are your correlative
   body! O it, more than all else, you delight-
   ing,

where his word-adducing transcends all recognizable grammar and metaphor and becomes a sort of abortive verbal algebra. And the self cannot mediate between the concrete and the abstract when, as but too frequently happens, it is absorbed into the abstract. But in "Song of Myself" these errors are mostly avoided, and it is in this poem that Whitman's peculiar poetic devices work best.

Suggestions for Additional Reading

An excellent general account of Whitman's life and poetic development is G. W. Allen's *The Solitary Singer* (New York, 1955). Two early books that provide close-up, if not always reliable, pictures of the poet are R. M. Bucke's *Walt Whitman* (Philadelphia, 1883), and H. Traubel, *With Walt Whitman in Camden*, 3 vols. (Boston, 1906; New York, 1908; New York, 1914).

There are several collections of primary materials useful for illuminating Whitman's relations to American society. *The Gathering of the Forces*, 2 vols. (New York, 1920), is a collection of editorials, essays, literary and dramatic reviews, and other materials written by Whitman as editor of the *Brooklyn Daily Eagle* in 1846 and 1847, and edited by C. Rodgers and J. Black. A collection of Whitman's editorials (from the *Brooklyn Daily Times*) is *I Sit and Look Out* (New York, 1932), edited by E. Holloway and V. Schwarz. E. Holloway also edited the *Uncollected Poetry and Prose of Walt Whitman*, 2 vols. (New York, 1921). Some of Whitman's comments on American society may be found in *Walt Whitman's Workshop* (Cambridge, Massachusetts, 1928), a collection of unpublished manuscripts edited by C. J. Furness. J. L. Blau places Whitman's political views in the Jacksonian context in *Social Theories of Jacksonian Democracy* (New York, 1947), a collection of representative writings of the period 1825–1850.

A number of scholars stress Whitman's relations to his age. Newton Arvin's *Whitman* (New York, 1938) reveals the incipient socialist tendency in Whitman's thought. Van Wyck Brooks recreates the intellectual and literary situation in *The Times of Melville and Whitman* (New York, 1947). The links between Whitman's use of the vernacular, Mark Twain's style, and the political assumptions underlying the work of both men have been suggested by Leo Marx in "The Vernacular Tradition in American Literature," *Studies in American Culture,* eds. J. J. Kwiat and M. C. Turpie (Minneapolis, 1960), pp. 109–122. In *American Renaissance* (New York, 1941), F. O. Matthiessen sets Whitman's commitment to democratic values against the work of Emerson, Thoreau, Hawthorne, and Melville. Lewis Mumford's account of Whitman in *The Golden Day* (New York, 1926) also is valuable. V. L. Parrington treats Whitman as embodying the "Afterglow of the Enlightenment" in the third volume of his *Main Currents in American Thought,* 3 vols. (New York, 1927, 1930). Mrs. Alice L. Cooke has revealed "Whitman's Indebtedness to the Scientific Thought of His Day," in The University of Texas *Studies in English,* XIV, 115–124 (July, 1936). Students interested in Whitman's debt to Emerson should consult Edmund Wilson's collection of documents on their relations, "Emerson and Whitman" in *The Shock of Recognition* (New York, 1943), pp. 244–295. An interesting chapter in Whitman's political thought is discussed by G. Paine, "The Literary Relations of Whitman and Carlyle, with Especial Reference to their Contrasting Views of Democracy," *Studies in Philology,* XXXVI, 550–563 (July, 1939). A provocative Soviet view of Whitman is D. S. Mirsky's "Walt Whitman: Poet of American Democracy," translated by B. G. Guerney in *Dialectics*

(Critics Group), No. 1, 1937, pp. 11–29.

There are many interesting critical evaluations of Whitman's work. A French scholar, R. Asselineau, has traced the development of Whitman's poetry after 1855 in *L'évolution de Walt Whitman* (Paris, 1954). Malcolm Cowley has edited an authoritative version of *Leaves of Grass,* the first (1855) edition (New York, 1959), with an excellent introduction and notes. In 1955, the centenary of the first edition, M. Hindus edited *Leaves of Grass, One Hundred Years After* (Stanford, 1955), a collection of new essays by several writers including William Carlos Williams, Kenneth Burke, David Daiches, J. Middleton Murry, and Leslie Fiedler. Fiedler's essay, "Images of Walt Whitman," is particularly relevant to the issues raised in the present volume. James E. Miller, Jr., treats "Song of Myself" as an "inverted mystical experience" in *A Critical Guide to Leaves of Grass* (Chicago, 1957). Constance Rourke was the first to regard Whitman as in any sense a humorous poet. Her study, *American Humor* (New York, 1931), includes Whitman in the tradition of native comedy. J. A. Symonds' *Walt Whitman, A Study* (London, 1893), was the first serious analysis of Whitman's work, and remains invaluable. The *Walt Whitman Handbook* (Chicago, 1946), edited by G. W. Allen, categorizes all the writings by and about Whitman before 1945. For more recent work see the quarterly bibliography of "Articles on American Literature Appearing in Current Periodicals," which is published in each issue of the journal, *American Literature,* Duke University Press, Durham, North Carolina.

4 5 6 7 8 9 10